SOME OF THE WHIMSY, SUPERSTITIONS, PHRASES, AND BELIEFS EXPLORED IN *ANIMAL FOLKLORE*

- A cat has nine lives
- Never kill a spider
- A bird in the hand is worth two in the bush
- Ancient medicine and treatment
- Toadying behavior
- The raven is a sign of death
- Stubborn as a mule
- The groundhog and his shadow
- The Egyptian sacred scarab

You'll find these and many more exciting, exhilarating, and extremely interesting facts about the animals in our lives!

Also by Edward F. Dolan
Published by Ivy Books:

THE OLD FARMER'S ALMANAC OF WEATHER LORE

ANIMAL FOLKLORE

From Black Cats to White Horses

Edward F. Dolan

IVY BOOKS • NEW YORK

Ivy Books
Published by Ballantine Books
Copyright © 1992 by Edward F. Dolan

All rights reserved under International and Pan-American
Copyright Conventions. Published in the United States by Ballantine Books, a division of Random House, Inc., New York,
and simultaneously in Canada by Random House of Canada
Limited, Toronto.

Library of Congress Catalog Card Number: 91-92406

ISBN 0-8041-0552-9

Manufactured in the United States of America

First Edition: June 1992

Contents

INTRODUCTION

Animals and Their Folklore

FROM THE EARLIEST OF TIMES, we humans have made the animals around us play a significant role in our lives. Our relationships with them have been many and varied—and, because they are relationships grounded in our humanity, rife with odd contradictions.

On the one hand, we have fashioned some animals into servants to pull our plows and wagons; on the other, we have turned some into companions to entertain us, ease our loneliness, or favor us with the uncritical affection that our fellow humans often will not, or cannot, give. Because we, too, belong to the animal kingdom and do what most all animal species do to each other, we have killed them for food; but unlike all other species, we have also stalked them for the cruel pleasure of killing for sport.

In our every relationship with animals—no matter whether we have been working, slaughtering, or petting them—we have watched them closely. Out of what our earliest forebears saw of their characteristics, their particular abilities, their sensitivity to the nature around them, and, indeed, their very oneness with nature, came a deep and awed respect—and out of that respect came the beginnings of the vast body of truth, half-truth, and sheer fantasy that we today call animal folklore.

Embracing virtually every land, sea, and sky animal, it is a lore that spans the entire history of human experience and thinking. In its earliest days it was grand in scope and almost wholly religious in theme, centering on tribal myths that used animals to explain the origins of our world. For example:

The Chippewa Indians of North America and the people of India and northern Asia all believed that the earth was created when one amphibious creature or another brought up mud from the ocean waters.

But those first theories of creation, as grand and imaginative as they were, served to explain just one of the mysteries of an all-too-mysterious universe. And so the lore became crowded with the attempts to answer riddles that stubbornly remain riddles to this day. For one, there was the question of how to heal the myriad illnesses that seem to lurk everywhere. Animals, because the ancient mind envisioned their marvelous oneness with nature as giving them supernatural powers, were made to play a part in early medical practice—thus beginning an association with both formal and folk medicine that has continued to this day—in the deep faith that those powers could cure. Two cases in point:

The Romans treated cataracts with a poultice consisting of the liver of an eagle embedded with balsam and honey. The Egyptians used a salve made of a frog's gall to ease one of the most common complaints of their dry and dusty land: sore and enflamed eyes.

But there was an even greater question to be answered—the question of what happens to us after death. The Mesopotamians saw a link between the freeing of the spirit from the body and the bird's ability to fly. For them, the dead took the form of birds in the hereafter.

Then there was that greatest and most bewildering question of all: who is it that controls our world and our lives? This bewilderment led to the concept of governing deities. Here, the animals did not go overlooked, again because of the ancient mind's fascination with the marvelous oneness with nature that assuredly gave them supernatural powers. Along with all the deities that came in human form—from those who reigned over entire societies to those of lesser stature who attended to specific human needs and on to those who were seen as demons doing Satan's work—they were given their fair share of sacred positions and godly tasks. To mention just one:

A number of ancient societies, among them the Egyptians, elevated the dog to god status. He was variously seen as the provider of light from the sun and moon, the protector against evil, and as a judge of human souls after death.

In all, hundreds of animals served as deities in antiquity. Additionally, there were those gods in which two or more species were combined, such as the feathered serpent, the blend of bird and snake that, under assorted names, was worshiped by the Mayas of Central America, the Aztecs of Mexico, and some Indian tribes in the American southwest. There were also amalgamations of animal and man, among them Pan of Greece. He had the torso of a man and a face similar to that of a human but the horns, loins, legs, and feet of a goat. His job was to make the fields, woodlands, and flocks fertile.

The number of animals endowed with a religious significance did not diminish when, in time, more and more societies limited their adoration to humanlike gods. The deep regard felt for animals would not allow them to be discarded. Instead, the choice was made to associate various of their number with the humanlike deities:

In pre-Christian Greece, the wolf was believed sacred to Zeus, the stag to Diana, and the dove to Venus; the Romans held that both the horse and vulture were sacred to Mars, and the lion to Vulcan; the Indochinese depicted their god of war as riding a peacock.

With the coming of Christianity, the associations quickly multiplied:

> Throughout Europe, though not considered sacred in themselves, the bird has long been associated with St. Francis of Assisi, the eagle with St. John the Divine, the deer with St. Henry—and so on until the list strikes one as endless. In Sweden the stork was (and still is) held sacred because of an odd link with Jesus Christ.

Over the centuries, as new religious concepts replaced the earliest attempts to explain creation and the forces governing our world, animal folklore lost its original grand themes in all but the most primitive societies. Now it became a body of sayings, proverbs, outlooks, and superstitions that were concocted mainly by the common people. While lacking the grandeur of a bygone day, it nevertheless remained a treasure trove of imaginative thinking that touched all aspects of everyday life.

It spoke, for instance, of our perennial yearning to know what the future holds so that we can somehow prepare ourselves to endure or manipulate it. Here, revealing the pessimistic and frightened side of human nature, our forebears gave the lore such still-remembered commonplace omens of approaching ill fortune as:

> When a dog howls in the night, someone nearby has died or will soon die.

But, since our nature also has an optimistic side, the lore came to have its full share of indications of good fortune—in the workplace, at home, and in matters of the heart—looming just beyond the horizon:

> Carry eggs into your fields at planting time and place them in the ground with your seeds. They will charm nature into giving you a rich harvest.

It's a sign of good luck, when a cricket comes to live in your house.

When you glimpse a redbird, you'll soon receive a love letter.

Not content with looking on the animals as signs of things to come, our forebears went a step further. They used them as insurance policies against ill fortune:

For good luck all year round, be sure to eat hog jowls and black-eyed peas on New Year's Day.

—American Ozarks

Carry a rabbit's foot at all times for good luck.

On a more practical level, generation after generation filled the lore with predictions of the future based on animal behaviors at certain times. Many of these predictions had to do with the weather and came mostly from people who made their living on the land. Constantly aware of what the changing weather could do to nourish or destroy their crops, they saw—or thought they saw—a connection between the actions of their livestock and the coming of rain, snow, or fair skies. Hence, such still-cherished rhymed admonitions as:

A cow with its tail to the west
Makes weather the best.
A cow with its tail to the east
Makes weather the least.

Possibly the most amusing—and certainly among the most familiar—contributions to the lore have come from our age-old ability to see the link between human features, traits, and behaviors and those of animals. We know exactly what past generations meant when they first described someone as ''giraffe-necked'' and ''stubborn as a mule.'' And we can pretty well guess the human characteristics and behaviors implied in such no longer widely familiar observations as:

The whiter the cow, the surer it is to go to the altar.

A cat may look at a king.

Bees that have honey in their mouths have stings in their tails.

He who keeps company with the wolf will learn to howl.

With its host of sayings, proverbs, symbols, and superstitions, the lore remains with us today. But after centuries of passing, so often by word of mouth, from generation to generation, only remnants of it have reached us. Along the way some of the most fascinating information that it has to offer has been generally forgotten. Who among us knows, for instance, why the universally feared and so often deadly snake has found its way into the caduceus, the symbol of the medical profession with its commitment to saving lives?

Unfortunately, so many of the remnants that still linger on the scene are superstitions that the majority of us dismiss with disdain or amusement. We are, so we tell ourselves, the products of enlightened times. We know better than to believe that a plate of hog jowls on New Year's Day really ensures twelve months of good luck or that a black cat crossing one's path will certainly bring misfortune.

It is true that, in some ways at least, we are more enlightened than our forebears. And true that many of the superstitions are plain silly. But it is a sad mistake to dismiss the lore simply as a collection of groundless beliefs and practices handed down to us by ancestors less wise and sophisticated than we. To do so is to turn our backs on a set of outlooks and activities that may have started as a quest for a better understanding and appreciation of the animals around us, but ended up speaking volumes about our own natures—about our way of thinking and believing; about our ability to observe and make connections (either valid or totally off the mark, but nevertheless connections) between apparently unrelated facts; about our fear of the unknown and our deep-seated yearning to discover and then somehow manage what lies ahead; and about our age-old desire to fathom our world and its bewildering ways.

In all, it is a lore that points up the searching intelligence and leaping imagination that makes our kind unique among our fellow creatures—a lore that, rather than revealing the animals to us, has revealed ourselves to ourselves. It's all there to see when we look at the myriad whys that lurk everywhere in the lore, among them the handful that have been mentioned thus far: why the Egyptians made a god of the dog, why Pan's job was to render the fields, woodlands, and flocks of Greece fertile, why the stork in Sweden is associated with Jesus Christ, why it is thought to be bad luck to have a black cat cross your path and good luck to carry a rabbit's foot, and why the cow with its tail to the west makes weather the best.

We live in a time whose technological developments have made us feel quite apart from all the generations that have gone before us. For all its faults our century has recorded more accomplishments in science, medicine, industry, and the production of creature comforts than the preceding five thousand years put into the books. But those accomplishments have lured too many of us into the arrogance of thinking ourselves distinct from the long and uninterrupted flow of human history rather than its latest products. It is because the lore has so much to tell us about ourselves by revealing how the minds of those before us worked—a revealing that can help us remember that no matter how separated from and superior to the past we may feel, we are still as one with it—that this book is being written.

To tell the story of the lore we'll look at the welter of beliefs, myths, fables, proverbs, and superstitions that has gone into its making, tracing them whenever possible to their origins, explaining why they came into being, and pointing out which of their number contain some measure of reason or truth and which, at the opposite end of the scale, are sheer but still magnificently conceived nonsense.

The great bulk of the lore that we'll encounter in the coming pages is of European origin. Some of its entries, on being born in one society, were embraced by others, while some, leaving little doubt of the commonality of the human mind, appear to have emerged simultaneously in various cultures. But more than a few of what we think of as European beliefs can be traced to Africa, Australia, and especially Asia, where they were picked up and brought home by traders. Most, perhaps virtually all, of the European beliefs were carried to the United States and transplanted here by our earliest settlers, putting down roots as strong as those established by the settlers themselves and making the United States, in its cities and countryside, a treasure house of "old country" lore.

Finally, we'll find that, as expected, there were beliefs and myths already here when the first European explorers stepped ashore; what was unexpected was that many of their number bore an uncanny similarity to those that were about to be transplanted from foreign seeds. Indeed, in the realm of animal lore, our oneness with the past is a oneness with the past of the entire world.

CHAPTER ONE

Childhood Fancies

Each of us was introduced to animal folklore at an early age. Perhaps the introduction was made by a great-grandmother or family friend who had been raised in a backwoods cabin or came from the "old country"; perhaps by an uncle cherished throughout the family for his peculiar turns of mind; or perhaps by the older and—by virtue of his size and advanced age—wiser kid down the block. No matter who was responsible for it, the introduction usually took one of several forms. Perhaps, along with such sidewalk wisdoms as "Step on a crack and break your mother's back" (an outgrowth of a vintage peasant belief that a crack in the earth is a doorway to hell), we heard some bit of information that added to the sense of wonder we felt for a still-all-too-wondrous world:

When you find an empty turtle shell, it means that the turtle has left it behind and moved to a new one.

When a bee stings you, it will die because it leaves its stinger in you.

A cat has nine lives.

Or we were perhaps asked a question that promised to have an answer too mysterious for us to guess:

Do you know why your dog has a cold and wet nose all the time?

9

Or, better yet, perhaps we heard an urgent and sometimes whispered warning with a deliciously scary feel to it. Who can forget the tingle that ran down a six- or seven-year-old spine on hearing for the first time:

Hey, watch it! Get a spider's web in your eye and you'll never get it out again.

Don't ever let a bat get into your hair. You won't be able to get it out unless your mom cuts all your hair off.

And, of course, so many of those first cautions had to do with good and bad luck. Again, who can forget one's first encounter with:

It's bad luck when a black cat crosses your path.

Carry a rabbit's foot for good luck.

On first encountering such old saws as these, we may have wondered whether there was a grain of truth to them. Perhaps we accepted at face value the ones about the spider's web and the empty turtle shell. To the young mind they seemed to make some sort of sense. After all, the web did have a clinging quality to it; only experience would teach us that it could be easily washed away or would simply disintegrate. As for the turtle saying, we would eventually realize that it was offered in kindness to protect us for a time longer against the harshest of nature's realities. The empty shell, of course, does not mean that its occupant has departed and taken up a new residence, but has died and decomposed.

Likewise, we may have accepted the saying about the bee because it, too, made sense. There, poking into the skin, was the solid evidence that our attacker had left behind what seemed to be a vital part. Today, we know that the saying has some merit. There are certain bees—the honeybee among them—that do lose their stingers and die shortly thereafter. The loss occurs because their stingers are coated with hooklike barbs that catch the skin and pull the stingers away. Other bees, however, do not give up their stingers and survive, perhaps to sting again.

As for the cat and its nine lives, here we were being introduced to a completely false idea that has survived since antiquity when, as we'll see in a moment, the cat was venerated as a sacred being in Egypt and elsewhere. It is grounded in the cat's physical agility and its talent for landing on its well-padded feet at the end of a fall and thus avoiding injury. One of the earliest-known references to the superstition is to be found in a fable thought to have been written some three hundred years before Christ:

> It has been the providence of nature to give this creature nine lives instead of one.
> —Bidpai (dates unknown; the narrator of the fable;
> may be a fictional character),
> *The Greedy and Ambitious Cat*

Later, in high school or college, we would find that William Shakespeare (1564–1616) knew of the superstition and may even have believed it. He gives us these lines:

TYBALT: What wouldst thou have with me?

MERCUTIO: Good king of cats, nothing but one of your nine lives.

> —*Romeo and Juliet*

But what of the other sayings, especially those that had to do with good and bad luck? If we did stop and wonder about their validity, it was probably for no more than a moment. I know that was the way it was in my case. And I think I know why. It was too much fun to believe them and ignore for the time being whatever beginnings there were to the skeptical side of my nature. My views may have been strictly my own, but I doubt it. I rather think they were—and, I hope, still are—universal among kids.

Nor did we likely give a thought to where they came from or for how long they had been around. Had we done so, we would have learned what was really happening to us. As was the case when we were asked why the family's pet dog had a cold and wet nose, we were being introduced to a set of animal folk beliefs, superstitions, and observations that would remain with us for the rest of our lives and that dated far back over the centuries.

The same holds true for our other introductions. Though certainly unaware of it, we were encountering a fragment of animal lore with deep religious symbolism the first time we glanced up at a rooftop and saw there a weather vane in the form of a rooster. And a centuries-old bit of the lore when we pulled our first prank on April Fools' Day. And some vintage bits when our language began to be sprinkled with such expression as "It's raining cats and dogs."

So let's do now what we didn't do as children. Let's see where the lore contained in all those introductions came from and for how long it had been around before it ever got to us.

WHY YOUR DOG'S COLD AND WET NOSE?

The answer to this question is found in an old tale told of Noah and the Ark. It seems that the dog has a cold and wet nose because he lent a hand in shepherding the animals aboard the Ark. When the time came for him to go aboard himself, the vessel was so crowded that he was forced to stand with his nose out in the open. And there he stood, exposed to the rain, mist, and cold for forty days and forty nights. Ever since, the noses of all dogs have never managed to warm and dry themselves.

A BAT IN YOUR HAIR

While anyone certainly might have some difficulty in removing the trapped bat, the belief is pure nonsense. It can be traced back to the Middle Ages and was a superstition initially limited to women. The belief of the day had it that once a bat became entangled in a woman's hair, it could be loosed in just one way. Her hair had to be cut by a man. That only a man could do the job leaves no doubt that the superstition came from a time when the idea of male dominance held sway. And the idea of the man cutting the woman's hair, intruding on and perhaps destroying her crowning glory, assuredly had some sexual connotations.

THE BLACK CAT AND BAD LUCK

Here is what has to be one of the most famous—if not *the* most famous—of all animal superstitions: the idea that bad luck lies ahead when a black cat crosses your path.

Along with being known globally, this superstition may also be one of the oldest on record. Its roots—though they initially had nothing to do with misfortune—can be traced back to 3000 B.C. when the Egyptians began to practice agriculture and decided that the cat, with its liking for the mice and rats that always threatened to overrun the Nile countryside, could serve as a fine protector of the nation's granaries. The cat's efficiency at this job—along with such traits as its uncanny agility and its aloof nature—seems to have been responsible for the Egyptians' deep regard for the animal. Looking on it as a creature of supernatural abilities, they venerated the animal and associated it with one of their major deities—Bast, a goddess depicted as having a feline head and the body of a human.

Though it was believed that she held cats sacred and was responsible for their protection, Bast represented solar heat to the Eygptian. Some historians think it probable that this representation and Bast's connection with the feline are linked to the cat's penchant for basking in the sun.

The Egyptian reverence led to a number of interesting practices. For one, cats that were the pets of kings and queens were mummified and entombed along with their departed masters. For another, the Egyptians based many of their decisions concerning state and family matters on the behavior of the cat—seeing omens for the future in whether the thing jumped in one direction or another, sat down or walked away, or chose to hiss, meow, or remain silent.

As sacred beings, cats were protected by Egyptian law from being harmed in any way. Anyone who injured or killed a cat, whether deliberately or accidentally, was subject to the death penalty. It is possible that the first association of bad luck with the cat—though not necessarily the black cat—can be seen here.

But this is conjecture. The fear of the cat is more clearly seen in Greek mythology, in the legend of Galenthias, the young woman who was turned into a cat and made a priestess of Hecate. Hecate, who was sometimes depicted as having three heads and sometimes as having three bodies molded together back-to-back, was the goddess of the underworld. In time she came to be associated with witches, witchcraft, ghosts, and magic. Though the Greeks disliked witches, the old crones were respected throughout the ancient world. The general view was that they were usually harmless men and women who were blessed with special powers. Those powers enabled them to do such helpful things as devise medicines, concoct potions to improve one's love life, and divine the future.

The fear of the black cat had to wait until medieval times before coming into sharpest focus. It was then that witches first fell into widespread ill repute in Europe, and then that the cat was definitely linked with them and, as an extension, with demons and the evil works of Satan. Stuck to the animal was the still-adhering label of being a bad-luck creature. Black cats were said to be the favored companions of witches, and witches were thought to be able to turn themselves into black cats. The black cat started on its way to becoming one of the chief symbols of today's Halloween, or, as it was then called, Hallowmas, the old festival that, held on what was the last day of the year in the Celtic calendar, marked the new year by welcoming the spirits of the dead and revering their supernatural powers.

Even today, there are those who still agree with the medieval belief that:

A black cat without a marking of some other color is a witch.

These unhappy views of the black cat, though ridiculous by today's standards, are understandable on several counts. First, the medieval years and those that followed (including the seventeenth century's frenzied Salem witch trials) were ones of deep suspicions and fears of the unknown. Second, the legend of the cat's link with the evil Hecate was still widely remembered, as can be seen in Renaissance times, in the mention given the eerie three-headed goddess in Shakespeare's *A Midsummer Night's Dream*:

Now is the time of night
That the graves all gaping wide,
Every one lets forth his sprite,
In the church-way paths to glide:
And we fairies that do run
By the triple Hecate's team,
From the presence of the sun,
Following darkness like a dream
Now are frolic. . . .

Next there were the animal's striking physical characteristics—eyes that glowed in the night, the ability to see in the dark, an uncanny agility, and a talent for landing on its feet and thus avoiding harm. These were traits that, along with its aloofness, had once won the cat respect, but that now engendered fear. And, finally, there was the color black. It had always been widely associated with the terrors lurking in the night and with that ultimate of all misfortunes, death.

Perhaps because the black cat became—and has remained—so firmly associated with bad luck, the white cat was early given a happier reputation. To have one of pure white cross your path is still regarded as an omen of good fortune in various regions of Europe and the United States.

A contrary superstition, however, is to be found in England. There, the white rather than the black cat is widely believed to be unlucky. This superstition may have been triggered in the nineteenth-century British imagination by the mummified cats that some archaeologists brought home from Egypt for study. The cats, all black, had been ones "fortunate enough" to be have been sent into the hereafter with their royal masters. Their color was the result of the drying-out process in mummification. All this, apparently, ended up giving the white cat a bad name.

If you were raised in rural America, you early learned the various techniques that could be used to reverse the misfortune of having a black cat cross your path. Many of these strategies were brought here from Europe and took root in various parts of the country. If you were reared in such regions as New England, Kentucky, the Ozarks, and Texas, you were early advised to spit in the road. Another recommended ploy was to turn around and walk nine or ten steps in the opposite direction or move backward across the animal's track. In other areas you'd go all the way home and start your trip over again, perhaps having something to eat before leaving. Or you might spit in your hat, turn around three times, fold your arms, or cross your fingers and, if especially limber, toes.

You did not have to live in a rural area to hear your fair share of suggestions. I was raised in one of the country's largest cities and early learned that what I had to do was hike up my trouser legs. My instructor was an old family friend who had been reared in upper New York State. She advised girls—at least in this instance—to lift their skirts.

Nor did you need to live in a rural area to hear that, should the black cat be carrying a kitten in her mouth at the time of your meeting, you were in for a double portion of bad luck.

Nor to hear the warning (suspected to have been devised by a cat fancier of long years ago, bless his or her heart) that you're destined for seven to nine years of misfortune if you kill a cat or kitten of any color.

On top of all else, there is a reverse of the black-cat superstitions (again, one suspected of having been invented by a cat fancier):

If a stray black cat—or a stray of three colors—enters your house and decides to stay, you're in for some good luck.

THE RABBIT'S FOOT AND GOOD LUCK

If the black-cat superstition ranks as perhaps the best known of the bad-luck beliefs in animal lore, then what of something that brings good fortune? The honors here seem to belong to the rabbit's foot.

This superstition goes all the way back to some of the world's earliest societies. The link between good fortune and the rabbit was based on two observations made by the ancients. First, the rabbit lived underground—a damp and insect-infested place—and managed to survive the dangers and evils there. Second, in a time when large families were desired for the help that children could eventually give in the fields, the rabbit was greatly admired for its procreative talents. In all, the ancients looked on any animal that could flourish in such hostile environs and still manage to produce so many young with so little effort as a lucky one. So why shouldn't it be able to pass some of that fine luck on to others?

However, if you were raised in the American south or southwest, you likely learned at an early age that the good luck promised by the rabbit's foot wouldn't come automatically on tucking the thing away in your pocket. You had to work for that good fortune in some very specific ways:

> For best results you were advised to hunt the rabbit down at night and shoot it. Not just any night would do. The deed was best done when the moon was full. Nor should you use whatever bullet was at hand. A silver one was needed.
>
> Then you had to cut off one of the victim's hind feet. The luck was in the rear feet because they were the ones the rabbit used for burrowing. Depending on where you lived, one hind foot worked better than the other. In some areas it was the right foot. In others the left.
>
> Finally, you were to dip the chosen foot in rainwater that had collected in a hollow tree stump.

When the time came to carry the foot, you'd be advised by your elders to place it in your left back pocket. If your trousers didn't have back pockets—or if you were a girl— all would be fine if you wore the thing around your neck.

And there would be one last bit of counsel: never lose the foot. The older it got—and the drier it got—the luckier it was.

Incidentally, you might also have learned that the ear of a Texas rabbit is also an amulet sure to bring good fortune—that is, if you take care to carry it over your heart.

And, had you spent your childhood in England, you

likely would have heard that the very mention of "rabbit" or "white rabbit" has the power to generate good fortune. All that you needed to do was speak either term aloud one or three times early in the morning of the first day of the month. However, if everything was to work as it should, the term of your choice had to be the first thing you said that day.

As is true of the black-cat superstition and many others, the rabbit's-foot belief has a reverse side to it. Hares, a family of long-eared animals that closely resemble the rabbit and include in their number jackrabbits and "snowshoe rabbits," do not enjoy a reputation for good luck. An idea that dates back to the Middle Ages has it that misfortune will be your lot if a hare crosses your path. Why? Because a belief of the day—and in the times that followed—had it that witches could turn themselves not only into cats but hares as well. English dramatist Ben Jonson (1572–1637), in his play *The Sad Shepherd*, written shortly before his death, had one of his characters go so far as to say:

A witch is a kind of hare.

THE WEATHER VANE AND THE ROOSTER

The weather vane itself is of ancient origin, with one of its earliest mentions being found in the first-century-B.C. works of the Roman engineer and architect Vitruvius Pollio, who called it a *triton*. For many centuries the vane was placed atop towers and castle battlements and was customarily in the form of a banner. The figure of the rooster, a cock, was early mounted on Catholic church roofs not as a vane but as a representation of the cock that crowed at the time Peter denied Christ. Yet it must have served as a vane on occasion because a fourteenth-century verse, widely attributed to Geoffrey Chaucer (1340–1400), mentions a "wedercock."

It was not until the mid-1800s, however, that the vane

and the cock were combined throughout the Catholic world. At that time, a papal decree went out with orders that all church steeples now be adorned with vanes in the figure of the cock. Again, the figure was to represent the rooster whose crowing upon Christ's denial had so filled Peter with remorse. Symbolically, the vane stood for the Christian duty to repent and be on guard against moral and religious failings.

There was also a practical side to the use of the cock's figure. The large tail was well adapted to turning with the shifting wind, quite as well adapted as the arrow that had long been in common use.

APRIL FOOLS' DAY

The origin of April Fools' Day is uncertain. Because a traditional trick of the day is to dispatch someone on a fruitless errand, one theory traces its beginnings back to a tale connected with the Roman feast Cerealia, which was celebrated in April and honored Ceres, the goddess of agriculture. It seems that Ceres's daughter, Proserpina, was kidnapped by the evil god Pluto and carried away to his underworld realm as she was collecting flowers in the Elysian Fields. Her mother heard the echo of the young woman's terrified screams and went on the fruitless mission of trying to track down an echo.

In Christian countries the ruse of the fruitless errand has led to the theory that the day's origin stems from the moments in Christ's trial when he was sent back and forth between Pilate and Herod. A general theory holds that it dates from the time when March 25 was New Year's Day, with April 1 being the date that marked the finale of the new-year festivities.

Originally, then, the day had nothing to do with animal lore. Rather, it was known variously as All Fools' Day and Old Fools' Day. Several of the oldest almanacs in existence list it as the former, while one ancient Roman calendar designates it as the latter. Only later, in France and Scotland, did its present title and its connection with the lore take shape. In France, the person who was the butt of the day's foolery became known as a *poisson d'avril*, meaning the "April fish," the nickname given the mackerel, a fish that is easily caught by deception during the spring of the year. When it swims into shallow water. One belief holds that the term we use today for the victim of the day's fun—the April fool—probably began as an easy French substitute for the "April fish," after which it was borrowed by other countries.

And what of the connection with Scotland? There, the person who was sent on silly errands or otherwise fooled was long ago dubbed the *gowk* and his mission was called *hunting the gowk*. "Gowk" was a common expression for the cuckoo, a bird that suffered the reputation of being one of nature's silliest and most simpleminded creatures.

"IT'S RAINING CATS AND DOGS"

There are several theories on the origins of this all-too-familiar expression. One has it that our forebears early saw the obvious similarity between a storm's noisy fury and that of a cat-and-dog fight. A far more academic theory traces the saying back to early European mythology in which—especially in the continent's northern regions—the cat symbolized and influenced the weather, and the dog the wind. Then, as some folklorists suspect, the whole idea may have taken shape in the Great Britain of several hundred years ago when rainstorms left the streets flowing with debris, sewage, and the bodies of dead animals, among them those of cats and dogs.

Whatever its true origins may be, it is an old saw that refuses to die. We first heard it as children, and we can be sure that our children's children will one day hear it. Further, it is just one of many expressions that have been inspired by the looks, behaviors, and traits of the animals around us.

COLLECTIBLES

Cats and Dogs

ANIMAL SAYINGS are found in all languages and certainly total in the hundreds, if not somewhere in the thousands. Their number is so great and the ideas behind them so varied that it is impossible to fit them all into the areas covered within the chapters of this book. So that they and the richness they have contributed to the lore will not be overlooked, here is the first of seven collections of comments, beliefs, proverbs, and rhymes that resist the idea of being chapter topics. Each collection focuses on a specific group of animals. There will be brief explanations of those entries whose meanings are not readily apparent. For your enjoyment and browsing along the way, the collections are placed between the chapters.

Once a cat swallowed a ball of yarn,
And when she had kittens,
They all had sweaters on.

Killing the dog does not cure the bite.
                                                    —Abraham Lincoln

A cat may look at a king: An Irish and British saying that originally referred to peasants of a defiant and democratic streak. It means: "I'm as good as you are."

When the cat's away, the mice will play.

Every dog has his day.

He that keeps another man's dog shall have nothing left him but the line: A comment on the ingratitude of those in debt to you.

Funny enough to make a cat laugh.

To be made a cat's paw: To be the tool of someone or to be made to do someone's miserable task. The phrase comes from the fable of the monkey who, wishing to pull some chestnuts from a fire, used the paw of a friendly cat to do so.

A living dog is better than a dead lion: The lowliest thing with life in it is better than the finest without life. The proverb is found in Ecclesiastes.

If you cut off a cat's whiskers, it will lose its sense of smell.

A cat in gloves catches no mice: An admonition against being too cautious in one's business or personal life. Also a reference to someone who works in gloves for fear of dirtying his hands. A variation: *Muffled cats catch no mice.*

If you wish a dog to follow you, feed him.

House without a hound, cat, or child,
House without love or affection.

—Ireland

To look like the cat that ate the canary.

He who is of a mind to beat his dog will easily find a stick.

Before the cat can lick her ear: Never.

How can the cat help it if the maid be a fool: When an animal or a child causes damage or steals a morsel of food, it is the adult's fault for not putting temptation out of arm's reach.

All cats love fish but fear to wet their paws: Refers to a person who is eager to gain some reward but reluctant to work for it.

Every dog is valiant at his own door: A comment on false courage. The proverb is also heard with the word "brave" used in place of "valiant."

Let sleeping dogs lie.

Let the cat wink, and let the mouse run: A warning always to be watchful.

Like a cat on hot bricks: Very nervous, ill at ease in a situation. A variation: *Like a cat on a hot tin roof.*

> I had a little dog
> And his name was Rover,
> And when he died,
> He died all over.

CHAPTER TWO

Wisdoms and Comparisons

THE STORY of animal folklore is punctuated throughout with the invention of everyday wisdoms and comparisons in which animals are used to pinpoint human conditions, behaviors, characteristics, and physical traits. Many of these commonplace observations are as alive today as when they were first concocted generations ago. We turn to them constantly in our speech. It is more than likely that at one time or another, every one of us, when needing a word or a phrase that is both concise and immediately understood, has come up with something such as:

A bird in the hand is worth two in the bush, to advise an unduly ambitious or dreamy friend that a certainty is better than a gamble or that possession is better than expectation. The axiom comes from Miguel Cervantes's (1547–1616) *Don Quixote de la Mancha.* The British have a variation that was obviously first meant for the merchant: *A pound in the purse is worth two in the book.*

He's like a bear with a sore paw, to describe a bad-tempered person or a friend momentarily in a foul mood. (Sometimes ''head'' is substituted for ''paw.'' Anyone familiar with military slang and vulgarities will likely grin at either use. In barracks talk, another anatomical mechanism is customarily the word of choice.)

He's like an elephant; he never forgets, to compliment or criticize someone's prodigious memory. No one

25

knows when or why this one came into being. The ancient Greeks looked on the elephant as a stupid beast and the camel as the animal blessed with an enduring memory. All that can be said is that somewhere along the line, the credit for a stubborn memory was shifted to the elephant.

Dog-tired, to describe exhaustion; *bright-eyed and bushy-tailed* (usually a reference to the squirrel), to describe one filled with energy or a sense of well-being; and *like a bull in a china shop* to leave no doubt of someone's clumsiness.

He's living high on the hog, to comment on someone's affluent life-style or extravagant habits. The saying is a variation of *eating high off the hog,* which originated in the American south sometime in the 1800s and referred to one who could afford the cuts of meat found high on the animals side's. It was there that the finest bacon and ham were to be found.

He acted like a blind dog in a meat house, to describe (if you're from the south, especially Kentucky) a restless or indecisive person.

We are just as dependent on the animal world when it comes to pinpointing human physical appearances. Haven't we all fallen back on the likes of *pig-faced, giraffe-necked, hawk-eyed,* and *lion-maned* as descriptive conveniences? Most of their number have been a part of our vocabulary for centuries, with the same holding true of such words as *pigtails.* Today meaning the braids in which a girl's hair can be fashioned, it dates back to seventeenth-century England. There, it was first used to denote a tobacco that was twisted into slender ropes resembling a pig's tail.

In addition, every society has long had the tradition of dubbing relatives, friends, and public figures with nicknames based on some similarity between their appearances, natures, or activities and those of animals. Five well-known examples:

England's King Richard I, who spent most of his reign fighting the Third Crusade: *the Lion-Hearted (Coeur de Lion)*.

Charles A. Lindbergh: *the Lone Eagle*, an appellation dreamed up by the world press after his 1927 solo flight across the Atlantic.

General Erwin Rommel, the World War II commander of the German Afrika Corps, a genius at mobile warfare: *the Desert Fox*.

Admiral William H. Halsey: *Bull*, a nickname that had nothing to do with the physical appearance of this U.S. naval commander in the Pacific during World War II. Rather, it came from his ability as a 175-pound fullback with the naval academy's football team to "bull" his way through the opposing line.

Winston Churchill, Britain's prime minister during World War II: *the Bulldog*, a nickname alluding both to his physical appearance and to his toughness of character.

It seems as if virtually every animal species has served as the inspiration for a saying, description, or nickname at one time or another. And it seems as if those various observations—whether still fashionable today or long forgotten—have touched on most, if not all, aspects of the human condition. Here, to begin, are some of the things they have told us of human nature.

HUMAN NATURE

Unfortunately, more often than not from here on, we are going to be encountering some unhappy truths about ourselves, and so let's balance things at the beginning with an old European and American belief that at least in part has something nice to say about our natures:

> If we are able to make friends with a cat (or, in a variation, a dog), it means that we have a nice disposition. If the cat shows a dislike for us, take heed. We have a poor disposition.

The practice of using animals to point up facets of our nature goes back to the days when our ancestors were developing their myths and legends. In the behavior and appearance of many animals they saw, or thought they saw, attributes and failings that matched those in humans—strength and weakness, courage and cowardice, honesty and deceit. The animals were soon being made to serve as symbols of these human traits, with the bee, for example, coming to symbolize industry, the lion nobility and courage, the fox slyness, and the pigeon cowardice.

These personifications have remained with us through the centuries and continue to be universally recognized. We accept them at face value because, in part, the lion does look courageous and the fox sly and because so many of our views of animal characteristics come from our early listenings to early myths and legends—the Aesop fables and the Grimm and Anderson fairy tales. The odds are that we all still see the wolf, despite recent studies indicating his true nature to be much the opposite, as cruel and deceitful because of his treacheries in "Little Red Riding Hood."

As a result of all this, no explanation of the character being suggested is needed when we come up with such thumbnail sketches of someone as:

Gentle as a dove	Timid as a rabbit
Cheerful as a lark	Fierce as a tiger
Suspicious as a lynx	Brave as a lion

Proud as a peacock	Sly as a fox
Innocent as a lamb	Birdlike
Faithful as a dog	A lone wolf
Henpecked	Stubborn as a mule

The Irish seem to have a special talent for using animals to delineate human character. The woman is a favored target:

She's like a lamb (quiet and friendly)

She's like a sheep (again, friendly)

She's like a pig (sleepy-headed)

She's like a goat (a hurried visitor)

She's like a goose (sharp and pecking)

But the lore has given us far more than simple and convenient character sketches. It has gone a step further and has used animals to caution us of what can happen when two opposite natures collide. Many such warnings have to do with the dangers risked by someone of a timid nature when in the company of one of a stronger or harsher makeup. Some of the world's most distinguished writers have contributed memorable comments here, Shakespeare among them. He seems to have had a particular liking for the lion:

The hind that would be mated by the lion must die for love.

—*All's Well That Ends Well*

You may as well say, that's a valiant flea that dare eat his breakfast on the lip of a lion.

—*Henry V*

A lion among ladies is a most dreadful thing.

—*A Midsummer Night's Dream*

The lion, likewise, attracted the attention of Scottish poet Sir Walter Scott (1771–1832):

> And dar'st thou, then, to beard the lion in his den?
> —*Marmion*

As for other animals, the lore has come up with such wisdoms as:

To set a fox to keep the geese, a reference to an innocent who places his money in untrustworthy hands; *to cherish a serpent to your bosom,* meaning to assist or show kindness to an ungrateful person, and coming from the ancient Greek tale of the man whose gentle ways prompted him to pick up a frozen snake and hold it against his chest for warmth, only to have the creature bite him on returning to life.

To put a cat among pigeons, meaning to cause or stir up trouble, but also indicating that the timid person can easily be the prey of the predator.

He that is afraid of the wagging of feathers must keep from among wild fowl, an admonition to the timid.

The warnings have also included cautions based on hereditary factors and the inability to change or hide one's basic nature. Among the former are:

> The sleeping fox counts hens in his dreams.
> —Russia

Eagles do not breed doves.

From an evil crow, an evil egg.

He that comes of a hen must scrape.

Dogs bark as they are bred.

What can you expect of a pig but a grunt?

As for the inability to change or conceal one's basic nature, the best-known axioms certainly must be *you can't make a silk purse out of a sow's ear* and *a leopard cannot change his spots*. The former can be traced back to seventeenth-century England, while the great-grandfather of the latter is to be found in the Old Testament:

Can the Ethiopian change his skin, or the leopard his spots?

—Jeremiah

They may be the best known of the lot, but they are no more succinct than these folk wisdoms:

Cut off a dog's tail and he will still be a dog.

An ape's an ape, a varlot's a varlot
Though they be dressed in silk and scarlet.

The fox may grow gray but never good.

And two especially clever entries:

The higher the ape goes, the more he shows his tail.

You cannot make a crab walk straight.

Of the two, the former may need a word of explanation. What it means is that the higher in life ill-bred people attempt to climb, the more obvious their lack of breeding becomes. The latter is a common-folk variation of an observation made by the Greek comic dramatist Aristophanes (450–350 B.C.):

You cannot teach a crab to walk straight forward.
—*The Peace*

Of course, having been created by some pretty perceptive humans, the lore cannot resist commenting, at times gleefully, on the flaws in our nature. Consider the following straight-to-the-point commentaries:

On Conceit

Every bird loves to hear itself sing.

Every ass likes to hear himself bray.

On Foolishness

Fleas can be taught nearly everything that a Congressman can.

—Mark Twain (1835–1910), *What Is Man?*

If all fools wore feathers, we should seem a flock of geese.

It is a foolish sheep that makes the fox his confessor.

It is the blind goose that comes to the wolf's sermon.

When all men say you're an ass, it's time to bray.

On Greed

In matters of greed, both the hog and the pig, long regarded as slovenly animals with voracious appetites, come off badly. The former has been tagged as such in British slang since the fifteenth century. And so we have the insulting:

To hog it.

To make a pig of yourself.

Both sayings were originally—and still are—derisive references to eating more than one's share at the table. The former has had its meaning extended over the years so that it now also refers to a greedy nature in general or to someone who lives in rough circumstances. Likewise, two modern variations of the latter—*pig it* and *pig it out*—mean not only to eat too much but also to live in filthy circumstances.

In slang, the hog has always been identified not only with greed but also with selfishness and bad manners. Our own century has seen it provide two additions to animal lore—*road hog* and *hog*, the former meaning, of course, a driver of selfish, inconsiderate, and dangerous habits behind the wheel, and the latter a flashy, high-powered motorcycle or automobile.

But the hog is not the only target in matters of greed, as witness the following axioms, with the second being an everlasting testament to its inventor's rough humor, perceptiveness, or unadulterated bigotry (you may take your pick):

If the cat had a churn, her paw would often be in it.

—Ireland

Women, priests, and poultry never have enough.

BEHAVIOR

If asked to summon up an animal axiom concerning behavior, many of us would likely first think of:

Might as well be hanged for a sheep as a lamb.

A variation of *go the whole hog*, this old peasant saw has several closely allied meanings. As does the "whole hog" saying, it speaks of doing something completely and thoroughly and not settling for half measures. It is also used as an excuse to continue enjoying ourselves thoroughly at the moment even though we know we're going to hate ourselves in the morning. It further serves as a bolster against losing our nerve once we've embarked on some ill-advised or taboo path. The British have a nonanimal axiom that covers these same points: *in for a penny, in for a pound*.

While the "sheep-lamb" saying invites us to ride life with a loose rein, animal lore is usually more cautionary in its advice on human behaviors. Here are a few things that it has to say, beginning with those having to do with two all-too-human tendencies:

On Procrastination and Laziness

While the grass grows, the horse starves.

The sleepy fox has seldom feathered breakfasts.

Much of the advice against procrastination and laziness puts the accent on the advantages of action, diligence, and hard work:

Destroy the lion while he is yet but a whelp.

Lice don't bite busy men.

No bees, no honey;
No work, no money.

He that will deceive the fox must rise betimes.

And the most familiar of the lot:

The early bird catches the worm.

But there can be too much of a good thing. And so we have that time-honored warning by British writer James Howell (ca. 1595–1666): *all work and no play makes Jack a dull boy*. And, in animal lore, the following cautions, with the first advising against being a too-willing worker, the second against accepting too much work, and the third against trying to do more jobs than you can handle at one time:

All lay the load on the willing horse.

It was the straw that broke the camel's back. (Commonly, "last straw" is used.)

If you run after two hares, you will catch neither.

On Ambition

And what of the sense of ambition that drives so many of us to overwork? While *there's always room at the top* has long been a favorite spur for the ambitious, once again animal lore sounds a cautionary note:

> It's better to be the head of a dog than the tail of a lion.

> It's better to be a big fish in a small pond than a small fish in a big pond. (This one is often posed as a question: is it better to be . . . ? The answer is then left up to you.)

> In a great river, great fish are found,
> But take heed lest you be drowned.

On the Dangers of Flattery

A dog wags its tail not so much for you as for your bread.

As the wolf is like a dog, so is the flatterer like a friend.

Make yourself all honey, and the flies will devour you.

The first two proverbs warn that much, if not all, flattery is insincere, while the third cautions that flattery or a toadying behavior will eventually gain you nothing but everyone's contempt.

The word *toadying* plays an interesting role in animal lore. It refers to a *toady*, meaning a clinging parasite or, in modern slang, a fawning "yes man" or stooge. *Toady* itself has been in use in England since the seventeenth century and is derived from that ugly, rough-skinned relative of the frog, the toad, an animal then much despised by the British and widely thought to be poisonous. A century earlier, *toad-eater*, meaning someone so servile that, just to please, he would eat one of the loathsome creatures, had been the favorite term of derision for a flatterer.

For a time in later years a toady or a toad-eater was a young boy who assisted medicine-show doctors and miracle healers. The youngster pretended to eat—and sometimes actually ate—toads, which were still believed to be poisonous, after which his employer startled a gullible audience by ridding him of the poison with some magic elixir that the bogus medico just happened to have on sale.

There are times, however, when the application of a little well-placed flattery or even a dash of toadying may be wise:

Call the bear "uncle" until you are safe across the bridge.
—Turkey

On False Modesty

It is but a step from flattery and a toadying behavior to false modesty and the derision and skepticism it customarily triggers:

No man cries stinking fish.

And another short step to undue humility:

A little bird is content with a little nest.

And still another to false courage:

Hares may pull the dead lion by the beard.

And one more to the foolhardiness that can be born of false—or genuine—courage:

It is the bold mouse that breeds in the cat's ear.

To put your head in the lion's mouth.

Meaning to expose yourself to needless danger, this latter saying can be altered to read *to put yourself in the wolf's mouth* or *to take the bear by the tooth*. The reference to the wolf comes from the Aesop fable in which the crane witlessly risked the snap of the wolf's jaws in the hope of fetching out a bone.

Then we have a saying that dates back to Greek and Roman times. It speaks of the quandary of whether to cling to or let go of a dangerous thing or situation. One choice is as hazardous as the other:

To hold the wolf by the ears.

On the Company We Keep

He who lies down with dogs will get up with fleas is probably the best known of the cautions to be wise of the company you keep. Just as clever and to-the-point are these almost forgotten admonitions:

Those who play with cats must expect to be scratched.
                —Miguel de Cervantes, *Don Quixote*

He who keeps company with the wolf will learn to howl.

He who will steal an egg will steal an ox.

Watch out for the wolf in sheep's clothing.

The third axiom is a warning to avoid deluding yourself that the bad company you keep is really not so bad after all. The fourth refers to an enemy who presents himself as a friend. The caution to beware stems from the Bible story in which the wolf is able to creep up on a flock of sheep by disguising himself as one of their number. The same warning is sounded in the fable by Aesop (the possibly legendary Greek author said to be of the sixth century B.C.) in which the wolf dons a shepherd's cloak in an effort to lure the sheep to their doom—

and is echoed in later centuries in "Little Red Riding Hood," when the wolf disguises himself as the child's grandmother.

Then there is that best known of all adages having to do with the company we keep—the observation that those of similar character and taste associate with each other, and thus the warning that we will be respected or branded on the basis of whom we choose as friends:

Birds of a feather flock together.

Or, as it was originally written by British clergyman Robert Burton (1577–1640):

Birds of a feather will gather together.
                    —*The Anatomy of Melancholy*

On the Behavior of Children

The first two sayings here have to do with the fact that children seem—*are* is the more accurate word—always hungry. The last refers to a child's traditional energy:

Children and chickens must always be a pickin'.

A growing youth has a wolf in his belly.

Young colts will canter.

On the Child's Need for Discipline

There is not much in this category to please the modern, permissive parent. Most of what the lore says here was obviously born of the time when the counsel of British writer John Skelton (ca. 1460–1529) was still very much in style:

There is nothynge that more displeaseth God
Than from theyr children to spare the rod.

Skelton's thought was not an original one. There's no

mistaking the fact that he picked it up from the Old Testament:

He that spareth his rod hateth his son.

—Proverbs

Here now is the same thought in the down-to-earth language of animal lore:

It is the bridle and spur that makes a good horse.

Give a child while he craves,
And a dog while his tail doth wave;
And you'll have a fair dog,
But a foul knave.

The best horse needs breaking, and the aptest child needs teaching.

One that has nothing to do with the disciplining of children, but is certain to be as widely displeasing as any of the above:

A woman, a dog, and a walnut tree;
The more you beat them,
The better they be.

On Dealing with Others

The advice here takes several forms. To begin, in the tradition of *all that glitters is not gold*, there are these admonitions not to be misled by someone's appearance or attitude:

If beards were all, then goats would preach.

His bark is worse than his bite.

Next, the need for caution in your dealings with others:

Though the enemy seem a mouse, yet watch him like a lion.

Bees that have honey in their mouths have stings in their tails.

"Will you walk into my parlour?"
Said the spider to a fly:
" 'Tis the prettiest little parlour
That ever you did spy."
                    —Mary Howitt, "The Spider and the Fly"

Then, in the matter of protecting yourself against your own gullibility in your relations with others, the lore has this version of *fool me once, shame on you; fool me twice, shame on me*.

It is a silly fish that is twice caught.

And, finally, warnings to those who try to take too much advantage of others, for the lowliest of creatures, on being driven too far, will strike back:

Even the worm will turn.

Beware the cornered fox. (The name of another animal—dog or bear, for instance—is sometimes used here.)

On Going into Debt

In *Hamlet*, Shakespeare told us, *neither a borrower nor a lender be*. Animal folklore puts it this way:

Woe to him who has the cat's dish, and she's aye mewing.
                    —Scotland

On Making Choices

Here is the lore's version of *you can't have your cake and eat it, too*:

You cannot sell the cow and sup the milk.

On Being Content

First, with life:

Better a small fish than an empty dish.

Then with a gift or a good bargain:

Never look a gift horse in the mouth.

No one can say when this old—perhaps ancient—proverb was first voiced, but it has certainly been known in Europe for centuries. One of its earliest recorded uses is found in the works of the theologian and biblical scholar St. Jerome (Sophronius Eusebius Hieronymus, 347–420). A criticism of the act of examining a gift for imperfections and value, it is based on the fact that a horse's true age is best revealed by the condition of its teeth.

On Consistency of Action

Abraham Lincoln is generally credited with having made the following advice an American favorite:

Don't swap horses in midstream. (Today, the words "trade" or "change" are often substituted for "swap.")

Lincoln used the phrase, which means to avoid changing one's course of action or leaders during times of uncertainty or crisis, in a speech to the National Union League following his renomination for the presidency in 1864. Painfully aware that many of his listeners were disappointed with the federal government's conduct of the Civil War, he remarked:

> I do not allow myself to suppose that either the Convention or the League have concluded to decide that I am either the greatest or the best man in America, but rather they have concluded it is best not to swap horses while crossing the river. . . .

Though the press accounts of the president's speech gave the nation's colloquial language what has proved to be an undying addition, the remark is thought not to have originated with Mr. Lincoln. There are reports of it having been seen in print as much as a quarter of a century before he put it to use.

On Alternative Actions

There's more than one way to skin a cat.

There are more ways to kill a cat other than choking it with cream. (A variation substitutes "dog" and "butter.")

There's more than one way to kill a dog than hanging it.

On Anticipation

There's likely not a one of us who was not told at an early age: *don't count your chickens before they're hatched*. Famous though it is, it is not the only warning the lore gives us against the disappointment that can come of anticipation:

> Don't bargain for fish that are still in the water.
> —American Indian proverb

Gut no fish till you get them.

Don't sell the skin before you catch the bear.

Don't build the sty before the litter comes.

Don't eat the calf while it's still in the cow's belly.

The idea of anticipation ends this chapter and opens the way to what is possibly the largest and most fascinating of all the branches of animal lore—the assemblage of beliefs that has evolved from the human desire to know what the future holds for us so that we may be better prepared to meet and handle it. But first, another moment of browsing among the Collectibles . . .

COLLECTIBLES

The Feathered Ones

A wonderful bird is the pelican!
His bill will hold more than his belican.
He can take in his beak
Food enough for a week,
But I'm damned if I see how the helican.
　　　　　—Dixon L. Merritt, "The Pelican"

Don't you hear the bluejay call?
Don't you hear them dead sticks fall?
He's a throwin' down the firewood for we all,
All on a Friday morning.

The above rhyme is based on the old folk superstition that most bluejays report to the devil on Friday, bringing sticks for the fires of hell and telling him of all the bad things people have done during the week.

On the first of March,
The crows begin to search;
By the first of April,
They're sitting still;
By the first of May,
They've all flown away,
Coming greedy back again,
With October's wind and rain.

One beats the bush, the other takes the bird: Rarely

44

heard these days, this proverb means that the laborer does the work, and the employer makes the money.

There are no birds in last year's nest: A comment on the fruitlessness of living in the past. The saying is from Henry Wadsworth Longfellow's (1807–1882) poem, "It Is Not Always May":

Enjoy the Spring of Love and Youth,
To some good angel leave the rest;
For time will teach thee soon the truth,
There are no birds in last year's nest.

Kill two birds with one stone: To achieve two goals with a single effort. This idea dates back to Roman times and has been varied many times over the years, with the two-birds version believed to have come into use in the sixteenth century. The Roman comic playwright Plautus (254–184 B.C.) wrote of "catching two boars in one brake (a marshy area)." Later variations included *closing two gaps with one bush* and *downing two pigeons with one bean.*

If you see a buzzard
And don't see two,
You'll soon see someone
You're not expecting to.

Bird-walking weather: An old U.S. aviation expression, meaning the weather is so foul that even the birds have come to earth and are walking.

The bird is known by his note,
The man by his words.

A little bird told me: You've learned a secret from someone whose name you will not reveal. The saying had its beginning in the Old Testament and was intended as counsel against speaking evil of someone:

Curse not . . . for a bird of the air shall carry the voice, and that which hath wings shall tell the matter.
             —Ecclesiastes

To catch a bird, put salt on its tail: This bit of fancy was once the advice given to youngsters who wished to catch a bird.

It's a bad bird that dirties its own nest.
             —England and Ireland

Why art thou but a nest of gloom
While the bobolinks are singing?
        —William Dean Howells (1837–1920),
           "The Bobolinks Are Singing"

CHAPTER THREE

A Question of Luck

IT IS an age-old human tradition—the attempt to divine what the future holds for us. Still found in every one of the world's nations, in both the most primitive and advanced of societies, and extending back to our earliest fore-bears, it is a tradition that tells us much about ourselves—especially about our awed recognition of the mystifying forces around us and our deep yearning to shape our own destinies. Widespread and ancient though it may be, it is a tradition that is grounded in a simple but unanswerable question: what will we have—good luck or bad luck?

It seems that wherever our ancestors looked, they managed to glimpse some augury of good or ill fortune. For them, the most everyday of objects had something to say about the future: mirrors that broke promised seven years of bad luck; certain numbers were lucky and others un-lucky—"7" and "13" being prime cases in point; such household items as brooms and ladders could bring bad luck—brooms if you stepped over them, ladders if you walked under them. And, of course, the ever-present an-imals could not escape the questing human eye—not even the detested spider:

If you wish to live and thrive,
Let the spider run alive.

A spider on your clothes is a sign of good luck.

If you find a spider in your pocket, you will always have, or soon receive, money.

47

Daddy, daddy longlegs,
Tell me where my cows are.
Then I'll let you go.

The spider, as well as the tarantula and the black
widow, has always suffered from poor public relations.
Apparently, in the counsel to let him "run alive" if you
wish to "thrive," the country folk of old are telling us
what the entomological textbooks have long been argu-
ing—that the spider, with its appetites keeping the surrounding insect world in check, really deserves to replace
the dog as "man's best friend."

The spider-on-your-clothes superstition comes from
Ireland and signals more than an approaching good fortune in the United States, where it also means that you
will soon be getting some new clothes. And, as does the
finding of a spider in your pocket (which may be no more
than a variation), it can indicate that money is on the
way. The now rarely used term *spider money* has its roots
in this aspect of the superstition and means that the
amount of money soon to arrive will be small. These
associations of the spider and clothing with good luck
may come from the old European idea that a fever could
be cured by placing a spider in a nutshell and carrying it
about the neck.

The daddy-longlegs verse can still be heard in a number of American farm and dairy regions. There, should
your cows wander off, you're to pick up and dangle a
daddy longlegs and recite the verse. The cooperative spider will then turn so that another of its legs is pointing
in the direction of the missing cows.

Animals other than the spider also bring luck if they
decide to explore you or your clothes. European and
American women once felt certain that whenever a ladybug landed on their clothing, they would soon have a
new dress. Similar happy outcomes were promised by
other encounters: new shoes if the ladybug touched down
on your shoes, a new hat if the landing was made on

your hat. Everyone, however, was to beware of the dragonfly. Let it zoom in on the face and it would, true to its nickname, the "devil's darning needle," sew up the ears, nose, and mouth of swearing men, shrewish women, and naughty children.

Animal lore has always abounded with superstitions of good and bad luck, many of which remain in vogue to this day. They continue to be found at all levels of society. For the most part, though, they came of the people who lived closest to nature—the seamen, fishermen, farmers, and herdsmen—and felt themselves most influenced by the animals that were such a part of that nature. In general, the myriad superstitions can be classified beyond their promises of good or ill fortune. They can be placed in two general categories—those involving luck in the workplace and those having to do with personal luck. A few are able to fit into both categories.

LUCK IN THE WORKPLACE: THE GOOD

How to bring good fortune to your work? Our forebears dreamed up a variety of strategies. For one, the fishermen in a number of European areas refused to eat the fiddle fish. Rather, looking on it as a good-luck creature, they towed it behind their boats in the hope that it would ensure a rich catch.

For another, many European and American fishermen (both commercial and sports anglers) still think the odds for a good catch are improved by refusing to use the left hand to slip bait onto a hook. Many continue to observe the old custom of spitting on their bait for luck before tossing it overside. The farmers of Ireland also have long looked on spitting as an insurance policy against ill luck. Reserved for the birth of a calf is this traditional Irish wish:

God bless three times, and three spits for good luck.

And, for ensuring luck in the workplace, at home, or any other locale that comes to mind—there are these vintage instructions:

Spit into an open well and make a wish. The wish will come true.

If you're a girl and the hem of your dress turns up, spit on it and you will get a new dress. In some areas of the southern United States the upturned hem is a sign that you'll soon be kicked.

The practice of spitting for luck has its roots in ancient Greece and Rome. The ancients believed that spitting—on the hand, the ground, money, or an object—served not only as a safeguard against ill fortune but also as a weapon to help best one's enemies. The Roman author and naturalist Pliny the Elder (23–79) wrote that spitting protected one against witches and their evil doings.

But back to the men of the sea: British fishermen of old, after a meal of herring, never threw away the bones of the fish. Rather, they bundled them in a paper wrapping and tossed them into the sea. The fanciful idea here was that the bones would magically reassemble themselves into a new herring that would then call his fellow fish from the deep and into the fishing nets.

Scottish fishermen once practiced a quaint rite. They would throw a friend into the lake and then, pretending he was a fish, pull him in to shore. This was intended to let the lake fish know that they were supposed to imitate their human brother.

Now some examples from the land: the peasant farmers in several European regions carried eggs into their fields at sowing time and planted them along with the seeds, certain that the eggs would charm nature into permitting a rich harvest. It was with the same certainty that Slav and German farmers of old smeared their plows with eggs on Maundy Thursday (the day before Good Friday).

In Poland eggshells were suspended from trees to increase the orchard yields. All these practices were based on the ancient view of the egg as a symbol of fertility and, because it produces a chick that will in time hatch more eggs, of immortality.

To this day an old superstition persists among some European and American beekeepers. When the owner of a hive dies, the new keeper must inform the hive of the death if he is to have good luck with his charges. A failure to do so will see the bees either die or leave. The superstition was immortalized by the Quaker poet John Greenleaf Whittier (1807–1892):

> Stay at home, pretty bees, fly not hence!
> Mistress Mary is dead and gone!
>   —"Telling the Bees"

The superstition stems from the fact that beekeepers of old thought their charges to be quite intelligent. It was their custom to treat them as if they were members of the family. When there was good or bad news about the family, the bees were told about it. When there was a marriage, a piece of the wedding cake, decorated with a white ribbon, was placed in front of the hive. Above all, the family members were not to quarrel about their bees, for then the little things would not thrive.

LUCK IN THE WORKPLACE: THE BAD

Here, we return immediately to the sea and the men who sailed it—men who, because a sudden storm, a changing wind, or a suddenly dead wind could so endanger their lives, were quick to see good and bad fortune in all the things around them. High among their pet hates were the rats that have always infested the holds of ships. Sailors almost everywhere believed—as many yet do—that when rats abandon a ship just before sailing time, that ship is doomed.

The superstition evolved from the fact that a ship's hold was used to store not only the cargo but the vessel's supplies. Endowed with a voracious appetite, the rats were known to remain in the hold, gnawing away at whatever was in sight, until the ship began to rot and fall apart or ran into a storm or a rocky coast, at which time, instinctively sensing danger, they were seen scurrying out of the hold in search of some new haven. Shakespeare commented on this trait in *The Tempest*:

> A rotten carcass of a boat, not rigg'd,
> Nor tackle, sail, nor mast; the very rats
> Instinctively had quit it.

The seaman's fear of the rat was further grounded in the ancient conviction that both the rat and mouse were linked with the souls of the dead and consequently were blessed with insights into the future and were able to warn their human neighbors of death and misfortune.

It may be considered good luck to carry a rabbit's foot, but the animal was never mentioned to a seaman—neither while he was at sea or ashore. Any such mention was sure to bring bad luck, the worst of which was death, on a future voyage. Fishermen also feared the sight of the rabbit. To see one while on the way to your boat foreshadowed a poor catch or some misfortune at sea.

Why was the rabbit's foot considered so lucky for some and the mention or sight of the rabbit so unfortunate for others? The answer is that the rabbit was often confused with the hare, which, you'll recall, was associated with witches.

The fear of witches caused another animal—the usually admired cat (other than the black variety)—to become entwined with bad luck, at least for a time. British seamen and farmers of the late sixteenth century were frightened by the rumor of what some witches in East Berwick had done in 1590. It was whispered that the old crones had tried to raise a howling storm at sea by subjecting a cat to a series of magical rites, after which they attached parts of a dead man to the animal and threw the poor thing into the ocean surf. Their aim was to have the gale wreck the ship in which the hated King James VI was traveling at the time. The fact that the storm failed to materialize did not ease the fear that the ritual might work if the witches took it into their heads to try it again.

The fear, however, seems to have been a passing one. Today, the presence of a cat on board ship is widely thought to bless the vessel with good fortune.

Coleridge and the Albatross

For the general public, the best known of the bad-luck animals to the seaman is probably the albatross, the giant seabird that is found in the Atlantic and Pacific oceans, frequenting the waters around Africa's Cape of Good Hope in such great number that it has long been known to sailors as "the Cape Sheep." The bird itself is not considered unlucky because it is said to harbor the soul of a dead seaman. The bad luck comes when a sailor kills the bird, a superstition immortalized by British poet Samuel Taylor Coleridge (1772–1834) in his *Rime of the Ancient Mariner*, which was first published in 1798:

"God save thee, ancient Mariner!
From the fiends that plague thee thus—
Why look'st thou so?"—With my crossbow
I shot the albatross.

In the Coleridge poem the old Mariner recalls the two awful fates that befell his ship years earlier when, during a long voyage, he killed the bird after it had flown aboard and had been made a pet by the crew. First, the vessel was suddenly becalmed and lay for days in a dead sea while thirst slowly drove the Mariner's shipmates mad. At last, in vengeful anger, they hung the dead creature from the Mariner's neck as a symbol of his guilt. It is from this incident in the poem that we have derived the phrase *to have an albatross around your neck*, meaning to carry a burden—perhaps a guilt or a responsibility—so great that it prevents action or stalls progress.

Next, a strange, ghostly ship appeared on the horizon and made its way across the deadly quiet sea to the becalmed vessel. Aboard were the characters Death and Life-in-Death, who were throwing dice for the Mariner and his shipmates. Death won the game and, one by one, took the lives of all the crewmen except the Mariner. He was left to Life-in-Death, who ordered him to live on so that he could atone for the killing. On finally reaching home, the Mariner was forgiven his sin by the holy Hermit, but continued to suffer so much from the memory of his act that he spent the rest of his life wandering from place to place and speaking of the need to avoid cruelty and the need to love all that God has created.

While Coleridge's account may be the best known of the albatross bad-luck tales, it is certainly neither the first nor the only one. Though no one knows how far back into antiquity the superstition goes, it can be said that much of the idea for the *Ancient Mariner* came from Coleridge's fellow poet William Wordsworth (1770–1850), who had read *Voyage*, the 1725 book in which English privateer George Shelvocke described the bad weather that plagued his ship after he shot an albatross while rounding the Cape of Good Hope. British author Thomas James told a similar tale in his 1683 work, *Strange and Dangerous Voyage*.

Bad Luck Ashore

On turning to superstitions found ashore, we'll hear nothing of the albatross, but will quickly learn that coal miners shared the seaman's dislike of the rabbit. If there was one animal that they did not want to see while on their way to the pits, the rabbit was it. Again, the early confusion of the rabbit with the hare was at work.

Actors thought it lucky to carry a rabbit's foot in their makeup kits. But they were apt to come undone on finding that the amulet was missing. A loss meant a professional or personal misfortune lay ahead, possibly even death.

Farmers had, and some still have, an assortment of odd superstitions, some of which could be found practically everywhere, while others were restricted to certain regions. Five examples:

If you kill a frog, your cow will die.

When you move to a new house, it's bad luck to take your pig trough with you.

For bad luck, pull a pig's tail.

You'll have bad luck if you burn eggshells.

It's bad luck to change a horse's name.

This last one seems akin to and may be a variation of Abraham Lincoln's *never swap horses in midstream*. Actually, the idea of bad luck, professional or personal, attending a change of decision or direction plays a major part in other areas of folklore. We have, for instance, the admonitions never to change a gambling wager, never to change an infant's name, never to stir batter in one direction and then in another, and never to return home for a forgotten something at the beginning of a trip. Oddly, all disagree with the advice to change direction and walk away when a black cat crosses your path.

It is virtually impossible to say how these superstitions—and so many like them—took shape. One very likely answer is that most were born of some unfortunate coincidence. Someone once killed a frog and then suffered the death of his cow or toted his pig trough to a new dwelling and ran into bad times. That long-ago individual saw an eerie significance in the coincidence and told a friend about it, after which the friend told another friend—and, in time, a superstition was born and refused to go away.

PERSONAL LUCK: THE GOOD

Possibly the best known of the good-luck superstitions concerns the rabbit's foot. If so, then the following notion certainly runs it a close second:

> A horseshoe nailed over the doorway to a house or a room will bring good luck.

St. Dunstan and the Horseshoe

The horseshoe as a good luck charm can be traced to St. Dunstan, (925?–988), the noted British cleric and, for several years, the archbishop of Canterbury. A story has it that the devil one day visited Dunstan, who was well known for a variety of manual skills, among them blacksmithing, and asked the clergyman to shoe his cloven hoof. Dunstan recognized his customer, tied him securely to a wall, and then, pounding the shoe mercilessly into place, caused the devil so much pain that the creature at last began to scream for mercy. Dunstan agreed to release his prisoner provided that the devil would never again enter any building where a horsehoe was displayed.

It seems this was not the only occasion on which Dunstan bested Satan. According to another tale, the devil got his comeuppance when he tried to tempt Dunstan, only to have his nose grabbed and held by a pair of red-hot pincers that Dunstan snatched up from his forge. The saint hung on to the pincers until the devil agreed not to bother him again with his shenanigans.

Dunstan, whose talents included working with gold, eventually became the patron saint of goldsmiths. He has been depicted ever since as carrying a pair of tongs.

The good luck promised by the horseshoe is not limited to those hammered into place above doorways. In the Middle Ages people unfailingly picked up any horseshoe found lying in a roadway or barnyard because it was supposed to serve as a protection against witches. This idea dates far back into antiquity, when people regarded iron, due to its great strength, as a sacred metal blessed with the ability to protect them. For the Romans the god Mars represented iron and was depicted as the enemy of Saturn, the god of witches. In Scandinavian legend, the god of war, Thor, carried an iron hammer and wore an iron glove to help him throw the hammer. Whenever he threw the hammer, it miraculously returned to him.

One aspect of the horseshoe superstition—the widespread tradition of hanging the shoe with its two ends uppermost—has its roots in the very earliest of times and is likely an outgrowth of a belief concerning the crescent moon:

When the horns of the moon point upward, the weather will be fine. But when the horns of the moon are tipped to the side, rain will come.

The belief, totally false, was based on the idea that the crescent moon was a celestial bowl filled with rainwater. When its horns—its tips—appeared to be pointing upward, the bowl was thought to be lying flat on its back and able to contain its contents. But when the horns were tilted to one side or the other, the rain was certain to overflow. The same logic accounted for nailing the horseshoe into place with its ends uppermost. They then kept the luck securely inside the shoe. Otherwise, out it slipped and disappeared.

It is for this same reason that we are advised never to buy a toy or decorative elephant with its trunk pointing downward. The fact is, with manufacturers being as sensitive to buyers' tastes as they are, you'll likely find it more than difficult—perhaps even impossible—to find such an item with anything but an upward-curling trunk.

However, widespread through the practice of hanging the horseshoe with its points uppermost may be, not everyone agrees that it works best this way. There are many people in both Europe and the United States who argue that it should be nailed with the points downward. The reason: the shoe is then able to pull Satan up inside its confines should he ever venture through your doorway.

Along with the practice of hanging it above a doorway, a number of other traditions have taken shape around the horseshoe. In Europe and a number of U.S. regions, you may not use any old horseshoe for luck. Rather, as was the case for the people in the Middle Ages, you must come upon a shoe that a horse has lost. Further, its prongs must be pointing toward you at the moment of discovery. Then you must spit through the prongs, after which you may take the shoe home for its honored place above a doorway or throw it over your shoulder and walk away without looking back.

The Wishbone

You'll come upon a relative of the horseshoe superstition if you'll recall the last time you and a friend each made a silent wish (for a lucky something, of course) and then began to pull a chicken wishbone apart to see who would end up with the longer piece and thus have his wish come true. This after-dinner tradition is linked to the horseshoe for the simple reason that the wishbone (the animal's collarbone) is shaped like the shoe. Many of our ancestors credited the rooster, because of his talent for crowing before dawn to announce each new day, with having the power to foresee the coming day and, consequently, the power to see into the future. Since the wishbone resembled the lucky horseshoe, it is thought that the people of the day believed the bone contained the core of the rooster's foresight and held the magic to make a wish come true. In time, the superstition was extended to the wishbones of turkeys, geese, and ducks.

Or was everything the other way around? Did the horseshoe evolve as a symbol of good fortune—after which it was immortalized as such in the tale of St. Dunstan—because *it* resembled the wishbone. This may well be the case because the wishbone is known to have played a part in hepatoscopy, a medical practice that dates back some six thousand years. It called for the ancient physician to diagnose an illness on the basis of omens sighted in the liver (*hepato* = liver) of a sacrificial animal, usually a sheep, a goat, or a chicken. Once the diagnosis was made, all parts of the animal were discarded, with a single exception in the case of a chicken: the wishbone. It was carefully dried and preserved, presumably for the good fortune it might bring the patient.

A similar tradition was to be seen in Italy some five hundred years before the birth of Christ. Once a chicken was eaten, the wishbone was placed in the sun and left to dry. Then it was touched whenever anyone appealed to the gods for a helping hand with a wish or a problem.

More Good Luck

The horseshoe and wishbone have never wanted for company as harbingers of good fortune. The ancient Romans believed that it meant good luck to see a white rat. The Welsh brushed a newborn all over with a rabbit's foot to bring the child a lifetime of good fortune. In the American Ozarks—and elsewhere—there has long been the belief that a meal of hog jowls and black-eyed peas on New Year's Day will bring the diner good fortune throughout the coming years.

The Chinese have long said that a house will enjoy happiness if a cricket resides there; their faith in this idea is such that many Chinese families keep crickets as pets. The liking for the cricket is also found in Europe and might have been brought there by early traders returning from China. In what certainly seems to be a variation of the Chinese belief, many Europeans (and their American descendants) consider it good luck to see a cricket in the house and bad luck to kill the little thing.

For gamblers, there was—and, in some areas, still is— the European superstition that if you tie the heart of a bat to your sleeve, you will be dealt good hands at cards; most likely evolving from the ancient belief that the bat served well as a charm against evil spirits, the superstition was widespread at one time among the Hessians of Germany. An American gambling superstition, possibly inherited from Europe, holds that your luck at the card table will run high if you come across a frog while on your way to the game.

Even that scorned relative of the frog, the toad, is widely viewed as a sign of good luck in certain rural areas of the United States, as is the unfairly feared spider. If newlyweds catch sight of a toad in the roadway, theirs will be a happy marriage. Later, should they or any member of their growing family glimpse initials in a spiderweb near the doorway of a home new to them, they will bask in good fortune for as long as they live there.

In rural areas of both Europe and the United States there remains alive the belief that eating an egg, that universal symbol of fertility and immortality, is an act promising good fortune, especially if you wish to have children. Eating an egg with two yolks is doubly lucky; it promises to bless you with the birth of twins.

Not everything about the egg, however, presages good luck, a fact that brings us to the omens that can be called "mixed blessings"—auguries that combine both good and ill fortune.

PERSONAL LUCK: MIXED BLESSINGS

The egg qualifies as a mixed blessing because of the European superstition that you are inviting bad luck when you leave the open shell of a boiled egg upright in an egg cup after a meal. Rather, the shell should be broken, crushed, or turned so that the open end faces down into the cup. Otherwise, it will be invaded by witches or evil beings who will then get up to all sorts of what British writer Sir Thomas Browne (1605–1682) called "mischief." In writing of the practice, he explained that the intent of the diners:

. . . was to prevent witchcraft; for lest witches draw or prick their names therein, and veneficiously mischief their persons, they broke the shell.

—*Pseudodoxia Epidemica*

To See a White Horse

In England and the United States the glimpse of a white (or gray) horse likewise qualifies as a mixed blessing, with some people thinking the animal promises good luck and others hating the sight of it. In England the split in opinion tends to follow geographical lines. Many people in the north of the country consider the white horse a happy omen, while many in the south associate it with murder.

Why the difference? The northern view is said to be a vestige of the influence exerted for several centuries by the Northmen (Danes and Scandinavians) after invading the country in the late 700s. The white horse as a fortunate omen is said to be based in the local awe of old for the magnificent steed ridden by the Scandinavian god of the wind, Odin. The animal, which bore the name Sleipnir, was equipped with eight legs that enabled him to gallop faster than the wind.

But the regional memory in the British Midlands and south centers on the Saxon invaders, who arrived as early as the fifth century. Swirling above the heads of the locals as the Saxons advanced, reducing the countryside to ruins, were the banners of the white horse. Hence, the association of the animal with murder.

In the United States, the white horse is generally considered an omen of good fortune for a variety of reasons that have come down to us from continental Europe and that have outweighed any contrary view we might have inherited from central and southern England. For the Europeans of long ago the white horse symbolized purity, while the horse itself was much admired for its strength, its fleetness, and its alleged ability to see in the dark, a characteristic that soon had our forebears thinking that the animal could foresee danger.

Not every American, however, takes pleasure in glimpsing the white horse—and it is here that perhaps some variation of the central and southern British view lingers. New Englanders say that the sight of one after dark is a sure sign of approaching misfortune. To side-step whatever is to come, you must immediately lick the thumb of one hand and thrust it into the palm of the other so that the bad luck will be rubbed away.

Other Mixed Blessings

Most of the mixed blessings stand as a testament to our kind's stubborn insistence on seeing something bad in the good and something good in the bad. Here, to accompany the conflicting beliefs about eggs and white horses, is a selection of equally conflicting European superstitions that were early transplanted in the United States and went on to flourish here:

Bad luck is due when a rabbit crosses in front of you (as usual, the result of its early confusion with the hare), but good luck can be expected when the rabbit crosses the road behind you.

On glimpsing the first robin of spring, hope that it flies upward. You will have fine luck for the rest of the year. You'll need to worry, though, if it swoops downward. Then the coming months will bring nothing but bad luck.

It is a happy sign to have a bird enter your house—unless the bird happens to be white. Then it promises death. This superstition is still firmly believed in several U.S. regions where white birds are so unusual that their arrival on the scene is thought to be uncanny and a portent of evil.

It is also an omen of good fortune to have a swallow build a nest on your house. But do not remove the nest or destroy it. Then bad luck will surely be on its way.

You can count on good luck if a hen struts up to your door and cackles. But bad luck if the cackling visitor is a rooster. (More of the rooster and ill fortune in a few pages.)

If you are a product of the American south, especially Kentucky, the chances are that you early learned to be upset by dreams of a snake, for it means the bad luck of having enemies somewhere close by. But if you then dream of killing the snake, you should feel much relieved. It indicates that you have bested and defeated your adversaries. However, if the snake escapes, you are to be wary of others and take great care in your dealings with them.

And, were you a product of ancient Rome, though you would have thought it good luck to glimpse a white rat, you would have hated to find that he had gnawed at your clothes or working equipment. That meant bad luck (an obvious conclusion if there ever was one).

Black, sad;
Brown, glad;
White, good luck be yours.

This verse pertains to the spider and is saying that a glimpse of a black spider will bring sad news (obviously stemming from the age-old association of the color black with death and evil and, in the United States, with the poisonous black widow); the brown spider (because so many of that color are quite benign) means good news is on the way, while the white spider (presumably because of its rarity) indicates the approach of good luck.

PERSONAL LUCK: THE BAD

What of the omens of personal bad luck that have come down to us through the centuries? Let's try this one for a start: were you born of peasant stock in a long-ago

Europe, you would always burn the clippings immediately after your hair was cut. You would never allow them to be carelessly tossed outside. There, they might be snatched up by birds and used to fashion a nest. Then you would suffer headaches until the nest deteriorated. What was at work in the superstition was the ancient belief that one's hair was somehow linked to a person's physical and moral strength. That old belief is dramatically symbolized in the biblical story of Samson.

Then we have the following fancies. Bad luck will be your lot if you:

Dream of pigs. (Someone is going to ask you for money.)

Kill a deer on Sunday.

Kill a spider, particularly one with long legs.

Count the birds in a flock.

Hear a rooster crowing near your house or in the doorway of your barn.

Or as the Irish say:

A whistling woman and a crowing hen
Will bring no luck to the house they are in.
(The British version reads:
A whistling woman and a crowing hen
Is good for neither God nor men.)

The three things that Christ never intended: a woman whistling, a hound howling, and a hen crowing. (More of the howling dog in a moment.)

Again, as in the case of the workplace superstitions earlier mentioned, it is difficult to determine how some of the above ideas (and those pertaining to personal good luck) came into being, with coincidence seeming to be the likeliest possibility. It is easier, however, to figure out how the idea of killing a deer on a Sunday came to be associated with misfortune. For the Christian, Sunday was the seventh day of Creation—the day on which God rested—and was the day of the week when labor and other nonreligious activities were forbidden. To violate that taboo was to invite the wrath of the Lord.

The Death Omens

It is easier still to see the reasons, however misguided they may be, behind the following four omens of that mysterious, inevitable, and, for the majority of people, most dread of all misfortunes—death. We begin with:

The raven is a sign of death.

The fear of the raven as a signal of imminent death is thought to have evolved out of the bird's ability to sniff out dead and decaying bodies from a great distance. An old story has it that the Roman orator Cicero (106–43 B.C.) was warned of his coming murder by the fluttering of ravens and that on the day of his death ravens flew into his home and plucked the covers from his bed. There still exists in Britain today the old belief that when the ravens at the Tower of London desert their home, the nation will fall.

The owl tells of death to come.

The owl was once called "the funeral bird" because, as we'll see in a later chapter, it has the reputation of hooting immediately before the arrival of foul weather (which, especially in the medically ill-equipped yesteryear, so often brought illness and death).

Over the centuries, a number of strategies have been devised to thwart the owl's prophecy of death by making him shut up. In Europe and the United States you can quiet all the hooting by such tactics as taking off your shoes and turning them upside down, wearing your clothes backward or turning your pockets inside out, tying a knot in a handkerchief or a pillowcase, wrapping a piece of white string about a lock of hair, and throwing salt over your shoulder.

If someone kills a swan, he will die within a year, or if death does not come to him, then it will strike down someone nearby.

—Scotland and Ireland

The people in certain areas of Scotland and Ireland are repelled at the idea of killing a swan because of a lingering old belief that the graceful bird embodies the human soul. The swan, which has always occupied a respected place in animal lore, was considered a sacred creature in ancient Siberia and much of Europe. Greek legend held that Apollo, the god of music, was born of the mating of the goddess Leda with the greatest of all the deities, Zeus, who came to the union in the form of a swan. Legend also has it that Apollo's chariot was drawn by swans. In Norse legend, perhaps because the animal's down is reminiscent of wispy cirrus clouds, the swan is associated with Frey (sometimes spelled Freyr), the god of fruitfulness and of the rain and sun.

When you hear a dog howl, it means that death is in the neighborhood and will come to someone you know.

This superstition can be traced back to early Jewish lore, as was noted by the American poet Henry Wadsworth Longfellow (1807–1882):

In the rabbinical book, it saith
The dogs howl, when with icy breath
Great Sammael, the Angel of Death,
Takes through the town his flight.

—"The Golden Legend"

The association of the howling dog with death may stem from something as simple and obvious as his lonely and frightening sound in the depths of the night. Or it may come from a far more subtle early link between the dog and death. A variety of early societies revered dogs as sacred animals, often envisioning them as beings charged with guiding the human soul on its journey into the hereafter. The ancient Chinese, when burying their dead, often placed clay statues of dogs in the tombs. Carved into the backs of the statues were harnesses that resembled those worn by today's dogs that guide the blind.

Dogs were also widely believed not only to guide the human soul on its way to paradise but to protect it as well during the journey there. Some cultures thought that dogs received the souls of dying men and judged what was to become of them. The Christian era gave us the Hound of Heaven—Jesus Christ—who constantly pursues the soul and urges its betterment and is the Guide, the Healer, the Protector, the Judge, and the Light of the world.

The dog has one of the most interesting histories in folklore. Throughout the thousands of years that he has been known to be with us (archaeological excavations have revealed fossils showing that dogs existed as far back as the Bronze Age, whose beginning is roughly dated at about 6,500 years before Christ), he has been accompanied by two diametrically opposed reputations. He has been hated by several societies—among them the Jews and the followers of Islam, both of whom looked on the animal as unclean and the eater of garbage.

Likewise, when not treated well as a household pet, when eking out a living instead as a stray, or when cursed with a dismal personality, he has inspired such uncomplimentary expressions as *to lead a dog's life* (to live in want or to be constantly harried), *dog eat dog* (to give or be given no quarter in your dealings), and *yellow dog*. This last expression has come to mean a cowardly person—literally, a cowardly cur—and stems from an early industrial practice (outlawed since 1932) by which companies resisted the union movement. They demanded that their employees sign a *yellow-dog contract*, an agreement in which the workers promised not to join a union under the penalty of being discharged if they did so. Whether the companies who insisted on the contracts or the workers who signed them were considered the yellow dogs has been lost to history.

However, because of his habit of attaching himself to humans and often showing them an uncritical loyalty, the dog has long been known as "man's best friend," a reputation that was perhaps enhanced early on by a tale in the book of Tobit, one of the volumes in the Apocrypha; the story tells of how Tobias, when he embarked on his long journey, was accompanied by his dog and an angel. The Jews tempered their dislike of the dog with a certain respect, in great part because of the legend that as they began their secret flight out of Egypt, not one Egyptian dog gave them away by barking.

Further, a wide variety of early cultures—among them Egyptian, Babylonian, Persian, and Chinese—revered the dog as a deity or at least, as said before, a sacred creature. To them, he was variously the provider of the earth's waters and the light that came from the sun, moon, and stars. The Egyptians, you'll remember, associated him with providing their land's life-giving water because the annual rising of that brightest star in the heavens, Sirius, the Dog Star, coincided with the rising of the Nile.

For those not of a superstitious turn of mind, all the entries in this chapter may seem, to put it kindly, fanciful. Perhaps. Or, as the believers would say, perhaps or assuredly not. But there have been attempts to foresee the future that even the most skeptical will admit to have given us more than a fair share of omens that are anything but fanciful. They are the attempts of our fore-bears to employ their animals as weathermakers and weathercasters.

COLLECTIBLES

Of Field and Barnyard

The friendly cow all red and white,
I love with all my heart:
She gives me cream with all her might
To eat with apple tart.
  —Robert Louis Stevenson (1850–1894), ''The Cow''

An ass loves the sound of his own braying.

Pigs might fly if they had wings: A comment on a condition or plan that seems improbable.

Many a good cow has an evil calf.

He that wants a mule without a fault must walk on foot.

Cocks crow in the morn
To tell us to rise,
And he who lies late
Will never be wise;
For early to bed
And early to rise
Is the way to be healthy,
Wealthy, witty, and wise.

What's sauce for the goose is sauce for the gander.

Look to the cow,
And the sow,
And the wheat mow,
And all will be well enow.

There's many a good cock come out of a tattered bag:
The observation that one's beginnings are not everything.
The proverb originated in cockfighting circles, when the
animals were smuggled into the arena in sacks.

The egg shows the hen the place where to hatch: An
African proverb advising that the words and advice of
young people should not be ignored. The saying is akin
to our *out of the mouths of babes* . . .

Honey is not for the ass's mouth: An old proverb not
often heard today, this one advises that the best of and
most gently worded of arguments will neither convince
fools nor calm the angers of the unreasonable.

A wise old owl sat on an oak,
The more he sat the less he spoke;
The less he spoke the more he heard;
Why aren't we like that wise old bird?
   —E. H. Richards, ''A Wise Old Owl''

Till the cows come home: Never or a long while.

The goat must browse when she is tied.

A cooked goose: A person who has accidentally or stu-
pidly ruined his chances in a personal or a business venture. The expression has been extended to give us *to cook
someone's goose*, meaning to ruin another's plans.

*By their tongues people are caught, and by their horns,
cattle:* An Irish and British proverb warning against care-
lessness.

One sheep follows another.

The whiter the cow, the surer it is to go to the altar:

A British proverb saying that the fairer the maiden, the more certain she is to marry.

A visitor was shocked to see a farmer hit his mule with a two-by-four before ordering the animal to pull a load of hay.

"That was cruel," the visitor said. "Why did you do that?"

"Very simple, friend. I had to get his attention."

Oh, the Brown Missouri Mule
Has a copper-plated throat;
And the welkin (sky) splits apart
When he hits an upper note.
      —Arthur Guiterman (1871–1943), "Mule Song"

CHAPTER FOUR

The Weathermakers and Weathercasters

THROUGHOUT THE LONG CENTURIES before modern cloud-seeding techniques and weathercasting equipment came on the scene, all societies did what little they could to control and forecast the weather. They saw their efforts as vital because they knew that the livelihoods and even the lives of their people depended on how the weather chose to behave. Extended droughts could destroy crops and livestock and lead to widespread starvation. Sudden storms (or hot spells at the wrong time in the growing season) could do the same harm or dismast a ship and send it to the bottom.

THE WEATHERMAKERS

In the earliest societies the weather and its various aspects were thought to be controlled by special gods or sacred creatures, some of whom were animals or combinations of animal and man. Birds, because of their connection with the sky, the vast stage on which the drama of the elements was played out, early became associated with the weather. A number of people believed that giant winged gods were in charge of everything from the clouds to thunder and lightning. One such god for the Persians was Saena, who was depicted as having wings that resembled rain-bearing clouds. In India, the god of the wind was a creature with the wings and head of an eagle and the body of a man. The Chamaco Indians of South America envisioned the rain as being brought by birds with their bellies filled with water.

Among the earthbound creatures thought to have a sacred influence over the weather were the horse, the toad, the frog, and the snake. Persian legend told of the terrible struggles between the rain god Tishtrya and the demon Apoasha, who caused droughts; the former took the form of a noble white horse and the latter that of an evil-looking black steed. The toad and the frog, because their lives were spent in or near the water, were also associated with bestowing rain. Some societies went a step further with the frog and credited the little animal not only with providing rain but also with having given the world its water.

In those cultures that worshiped the tree, the people revered a constant companion, the snake, as the one who gave them all types of weather. Much the same kind of reverence was seen in India, where the snake was believed to control the rain, and is still to be viewed in two annual festivals—one in the country's north, the other in its south—in which the snake is honored by having its images tenderly bathed in and sprinkled with water.

There were other such rituals. An aboriginal tribe in Australia covered its people with the blood of their medicine man and then coated them over with bird down to make them look like rain-carrying clouds. In Mexico the Taruhumare Indians still perform a rain dance in which they imitate turkeys. To the north, in today's United States, the Hopi depend on their eagle dance to induce rain, while the Shawnees dip buffalo tails in water and then sprinkle the water over the ground.

The farmers of India and the Indians along South America's Orinoco River kept frogs constantly on hand as weapons for ending droughts. During dry spells they treated the little creatures like anything but the respected givers of water. They beat them with sticks, the idea being to make them so uncomfortable that they would let the rain fall again. The Aymara Indians employed a similar strategy. When suffering a drought, they removed frogs from Lake Titicaca, placed them in bowls, and carried them to a nearby mountaintop, there to be left on two altars. The day's heat quickly evaporated the water and caused the little animals to writhe in pain. The hope was that the rain spirits would take pity on them and send rain to relieve their anguish.

While some animals were beloved as rainmakers, others were feared because they were thought to retaliate with weather upheavals if violated in any way. The ancient Persians looked on one dog—known to them as the water dog—as especially sacred. To kill him, either deliberately or accidentally, was branded a most serious crime, one promising a drought that would persist until the killer was apprehended and punished. Once caught, the killer was made to carry twenty thousand loads of wood and was ordered to kill ten thousand snakes, ten thousand cats, and ten thousand flies and earthworms. He was also tied down and had his back lashed twenty thousand times.

On a happier note a number of animals continue to be looked on as excellent weather prophets. An early American Indian belief has it that when the buffalo's hide is thick, the coming winter will be especially cold. A still-popular theory that can been traced back to ancient Greece and Rome holds that the pig can sniff changes in the wind and smell a coming rain. In Europe the bear and badger—and in the United States, the groundhog—have been used for generations to determine whether the winter is to end soon or continue for a number of weeks.

These prophets bring us to one of the most fascinating aspects of all folklore—the centuries-old use of animals to forecast what harm or good the weather plans to do in the next hours, days, or weeks. It is a practice that has resulted in a collection of folk predictions that range from the uncannily accurate to the completely false.

THE WEATHERCASTERS

To discover some clue of the harm or good that lay over the horizon, our forebears, especially those whose welfare most depended on the nature around them—the farmers, herdsmen, and seamen—looked in three directions: to the sky with its clouds and various tints; to the land with its plants and trees; and to the family's livestock and pets. Whenever they sighted a repeated phenomenon that suggested a coming change in the weather, they fashioned a prediction around it that was then passed along, customarily by word of mouth, from generation to generation. Since they were to be transmitted orally, they were, more often than not, couched in rhymes so that they could be easily remembered. For example, from the family's livestock came this time-honored rhyme:

A cow with its tail to west
Makes weather the best.
A cow with its tail to the east
Makes weather the least.

The prediction is a sound one in our latitudinal zone (many folk predictions do not work worldwide but only in specific, though often vast and widely separated, areas). Accounting for its soundness are two facts. First, our prevailing winds come from the west and normally bring fair weather, while a hallmark of approaching rain in our zone is a shift in the wind that brings it in from the east. Second, the cow, in common with all sensible animals, grazes with its back to the wind so that it can sniff out predators coming from the rear. Hence, all is well when the animal's hind quarters are facing the fair-weather winds from the west, but when it turns its tail eastward, the watching farmer knows that the animal is responding to a wind shift that promises a change in the weather.

This and all the other folk weather predictions were

the result of trial and error. This is especially true of
those that are built around animals. For an idea of how
many—if not most—of their number came into being,
let's look for a moment at the farmer of old as he stands
in his barnyard in the hours before a storm. He glimpses
his favorite cow as she pulls some odd stunt, such as
rubbing her hind quarters against a fence. At first he
thinks nothing of all this, but then, in the next weeks,
always prior to a rainfall, up she pops with a couple of
encore performances. Now he nods sagely. This is more
than coincidence. Sure as hell, Old Bessie has some sort
of "weather feel" in her backside. With weather changes
being a danger to all, he tells his neighbor of what he
has seen. His theory soon becomes a forecast that will
be passed down through the generations, fanning out to
other locales as it travels.

Often, however, he would be seeing nothing more than
a series of coincidences and would jump to the wrong
conclusion. Or he would note the actions of one particular animal and allow them to lead him to a mistaken
generalization. But, just as often, his forecasts were right
on the mark. So, after long centuries, animal lore has
collected its array of predictions that range from the
true to the possibly true and on to the completely groundless.

Now let's see what all those shrewd but sometimes
misguided observers of a bygone day have given us. We'll
start with their predictions that are today accepted as
valid.

THE VALID

We begin with a venerable forecast that is considered
beyond argument:

Sea gull, sea gull, sitting on the sand,
Rain is due when you're at hand.

Along with a shift in the wind from west to east, the approach of bad weather is marked by a drop in barometric pressure. Naturalists and fishermen have long noted that sea gulls and many other birds do settle to earth when a storm is brewing. It is thought that the drop in pressure makes flying difficult. Adding to the problem of staying comfortably aloft may be the weakening of updrafts caused by the thinning of the air.

Also considered valid are these four old-timers:

Swallows fly low before a rain.

Flies bite more before a storm.

When black snails on the road you see,
Then on the morrow rain will be.

If the robin sings in the bush,
Then the weather will be coarse;
But if the robin sings on the barn,
Then the weather will be warm.

The falling barometric pressure accounts for the low-flying swallows. A number of animals, swallows and bats among them, are known to have ears sensitive to changes in air pressure. It is believed that in the hours preceding a storm, they swoop low to the ground where the pressure remains slightly and more comfortably higher.

Both the falling air pressure and another characteristic of an oncoming storm—rising humidity—are said to be at fault for those pesky flies. The lessening pressure seems to cause flying problems not only for flies but also for mosquitoes, gnats, fleas, and many other insects, and so they are inclined to swarm and then settle on any convenient surface, including our arms and faces. It is also possible that they swarm and bite because they are being made uncomfortable and irritable by the changing air. This would be the insect version of the suddenly painful knees that so many of us look on as more reliable items of forecasting gear than the charts and computer projections of the National Weather Service.

But what about that rising humidity that presages a storm? Here, we ourselves may have to share in the blame for the bites—though innocently. We perspire as the humidity climbs, with the odors we then release attracting the fly and his fellow insects and promising a meal as pleasing to them as filet mignon is to us.

The appearance of snails in abundance on the grass or along a walkway has long been considered a reliable omen of rain, perhaps because they are made nervous and restless (strange words for such benign, slow-moving creatures) by the changing air pressure and humidity. But a caution: their appearance does not invariably signal rain. They're happy to put in an appearance at any sort of dampish time, such as a foggy evening or in the moments after you've turned on the lawn sprinkler.

The robin prediction is both a forecast of rain and of either generally gloomy or sunny weather. It is thought to have come from sightings of the bird's habits in the autumn and spring. In the falling temperatures of autumn the robin could be seen perched in low trees and bushes while it sang softly, but in the spring it mounted to higher perches, among them rooftops, and sang more loudly. It may well have been sheltering itself from the growing cold in the autumn, while in the spring it was thought to be enjoying the increasing warmth, with the male also singing with greater gusto in an effort to protect his nesting territory.

A fellow flying creature, the goose, has been admired for centuries as a fine bad-weather forecaster. From the England of the seventeenth century comes this testament to the animal's value:

She is no witch, or astrologer, to divine the starries, but yet hath a shrewd guess of rainie weather, being as good as an almanack to some that believe in her.
—*Old Book* (a 1634 almanac)

Actually, the goose is the subject of predictions that have to do with the approach of both good and bad weather. Most center on the direction in which it elects to fly:

Wild geese, wild geese going out to sea,
All fine weather it will be.

This is an old saying of New England fishermen. Their trust in the forecast is such that, before setting sail for the day, they've long had the habit of glancing skyward to catch a glimpse of flying geese. Should they sight the birds heading seaward, they raise sail and follow close behind. Should they, however, as pointed out in the final lines of the following antique verse from Great Britain, see the birds heading inland, they call off work for the day. It is possible that the British verse was brought to the United States by our early settlers and that the New England rhyme is its grandson:

Wild geese, wild geese ganging to the sea,
Good weather it will be.
Wild geese, wild geese ganging to the hill,
The weather it will spill.

Fishermen also apply the same logic to the flight of sea gulls. And so the two predictions stem from the same root as the "sea-gull-on-the-sand" saying. All seabirds are apt to head landward when a storm is taking shape.

The bee's gifts as a forecaster rank right up there with those of geese. Any beekeeper will tell you that his charges, in an obvious reaction to the changing atmospherics, neither swarm aimlessly nor settle on some convenient surface. Rather, they return to the hive, bustle inside, and stay there until all is dry again. Their sensitivity has led to a wide variety of "bee poems," with one of the earliest having been written in Greece some three centuries before Christ:

When charged with stormy matter lower the skies,
The busy bee at home her labor plies.
> —Aratus (ca. 315–245 B.C.)

The next centuries gave us:

When bees to distance wing their flight,
Days are warm and skies are bright.
But when their flight ends near their home,
Stormy weather is sure to come.

When bees stay close by the hive,
Rain is close by.

If bees stay at home,
Rain will soon come.
If they fly away,
Fine will be the day.

And these epigrams:

A bee's wings never get wet.

A bee was never caught in a shower.

The bee is not the only animal to seek shelter and comfort when it senses a storm is at hand. Beginning with a lovely American Indian proverb, we have:

When buffalo band together,
The storm god is herding them.

When sheep collect and huddle,
Tomorrow will become a puddle.

An open ant hill indicates good weather;
A closed one, an approaching storm.

While the buffalo and sheep may be drawing together out of a sense of nervousness caused by the changes in the air, it is also thought probable that they are instinctively closing ranks to take some measure of protection from each other. There is also the belief that rain is on the way when cattle lie down on going out to pasture. In New England and other regions it is said that they get off their feet because the changing air is making them feel rheumatic.

Ants have often been seen building and strengthening their living quarters during prestorm hours and then wrapping up the job by sealing off the mouth of the nest. Their activity has led to the belief that you can count on rain when you glimpse fresh earth on or around the ant's dwelling.

MATTERS OF DEBATE

While all the above predictions are considered on the mark, there are many that are the subjects of debate. Some people swear by them. Others—especially naturalists and meteorologists—seriously question their worth. A prime example here is the divided opinion over whether the pig is a trusted weathercaster and, if so, for what reasons. For centuries British farm lore has given the credit to the animal's nose:

> Grumphie smells the weather,
> An' Grumphie sees the wun' [the wind],
> He kens when clouds will gather
> An' smoor [hide] the blinkin' sun.

In the rhyme ''sees'' serves as a substitute for ''smells'' or ''senses.'' Those who question the prediction doubt that the pig's nose has any particular talent for sniffing out changes in the weather; there is no evidence, they argue, to prove the animal's olfactory abilities. Rather, they believe that the pig may simply be giving an impression of sniffing because it is tossing its snout in agitation over the changing air pressure and humidity. The tossing snout is accompanied by another behavior—

the chewing of straw—that indicates a growing state of nervousness:

> When pigs carry sticks [straws in their mouths]
> The clouds will play tricks.
> When they lie in the mud,
> No fears of floods.

> —Great Britain

The Roman poet Virgil (70–19 B.C.) commented on the same behavior:

> Swine are not heedful to toss about with their snouts the loosened wisps [straws].

Long before Virgil there was the already-mentioned Greek poet Aratus. He warned to expect rain when you see "swine in miry litter wallowing." Aratus is not here contradicting the British counsel to have "no fears of flood" when pigs are lying in the mud. The British wording indicates a tranquil mood, while the Greek poet's "wallowing" suggests a state of turmoil.

An old saying about ants is likewise a subject of much doubt:

> When ants travel in a straight line, expect rain;
> When they scatter, expect fair weather.

The problem here is that we are dealing with an inconsistent behavior that lacks any real evidence to connect it with a coming rain. Some ants have been seen heading back to their nest in a straight line before a rain. Others have returned home in scattered formations. Need any householder be told of how ants can scurry along a kitchen countertop in a perfectly straight line during the best of weathers? In a number of regions the "straight line" prediction has been extended to include all types of bugs and is generally conceded to be false.

Next comes a prediction that suffers in the same way as the one above. It, too, deals with an inconsistent behavior that may have no connection with the bad weather:

If the cock crows on going to bed,
He wakens with a watery head.

Some roosters have been heard to crow at night, an unaccustomed time for them to make noise, before a storm. But others have kept their mouths shut. If, as a storm is approaching, a rooster does crow before sleeping—or awakens to crow—naturalists are likely to say that he is being disturbed by the falling barometric pressure and rising humidity. If so, he is not the only animal to show its agitation by making noise, as witness these predictions, all of which have their supporters and detractors:

When the peacock loudly bawls,
Soon we'll have both rain and squalls.

When the ass doth bray,
Be sure we shall have rain that day.

When the owl hoots, the weather will be bad.
When he laughs, the weather will be fine.
                    —New England and the American south

The Cat on your hearthstone to the day presages,
By solemnly sneezing, the coming of rain.
                    —Arthur Guiterman, "The First Cat"

Also widespread in the United States and Europe are the beliefs that rain is at hand when:

Bats fly into the house and flutter about, making a great racket.

Crickets begin to chirp in the house.

Goats bawl, abandon the high ground, and seek shelter.

The bobwhite sings.

—New England

Yankee old-timers will tell you that the bobwhite's call itself is warning of the storm to come: "More wet. More wet."

The noisy animals are joined, so a great many people contend, by those that exhibit other peculiarities. The scoffers can do nothing to convince the believers that rain will not come when:

Mules shake their harnesses.

Calves run about nervously or gambol in the fields.

Cows refuse to give milk.

Fireflies appear in great number.

Spiders abandon their webs.

Frogs gather close to the house (and, joining the noisy animals, set to croaking in ditches).

Cats wash their faces.

Dogs eat grass.

The final two entries need a word of comment. When your cat begins to wash itself, New Englanders say that you can tell the direction from which the storm is approaching by watching the direction the cat is facing and the paw being used for the washing. Say that the animal is washing with the right paw while facing north. The wind is blowing out of the northeast and the rain can be expected from that direction. Or so the New Englanders say.

Though widely disputed, the idea that dogs eat grass before a rain is thought by some naturalists to have merit when applied to old, stiff-jointed dogs. The changing barometric pressure may be making the animals ill, with the dogs then stuffing themselves with grass to induce vomiting in the hope of easing their discomfort.

Whether true or false, the prediction is one of the most famous in animal lore because of its connection with Edward Jenner (1749–1823), the British doctor who devised the world's first workable vaccine against smallpox. An ardent naturalist as well as a physician, Jenner is the author of the poem ''Signs of Rain,'' in which he wrote:

> My dog, so altered in his taste,
> Quits mutton bones on grass to feast.

Dr. Jenner did not stop at the mention of his dog. The poem is sprinkled throughout with predictions based on the animal behaviors that he saw for years in the fields and woods surrounding his home in rural southwest England. In fact, he managed to put into the poem most of the forecasts that have been mentioned in this chapter:

> Loud quacks the duck, the peacocks cry . . .
> And see yon rooks, how odd their flight,
> They imitate the gliding kite,
> Or seem precipitate to fall
> As if they felt the piercing ball;
> How restless are the snorting swine,
> The busy flies disturb the kine,
> Low o'er the grass the swallow wings,
> The cricket, too, how sharp he sings. . . .
> Through the clear streams the fishes rise,
> And nimbly catch the incautious flies. . . .

The doctor's mention of fish brings us to two forecasts for the sportsman that have long been hotly debated:

> Near the surface, quick to bite,
> Catch your fish when rain's in sight.

Fish bite the least,
With wind in the east.

Since an east wind is a classic symptom of approaching bad weather in our latitudes, the two forecasts contradict each other. The first seems truer because we know today that both fresh- and saltwater fish tend to move closer to the surface in prestorm hours. The theory is that the move is prompted by a change in the distribution of the water's oxygen content due to the drop in barometric pressure.

But is the second prediction then false? There is no way of telling. All depends on the fishermen you happen to meet. Some will tell you that fish do bite more readily before than after a storm. Others will argue that the rising fish have no interest in taking your bait but instead prefer snapping at the flies and other insects that swarm close to the water.

It is also possible that the second prediction refers to the coming of a thunderstorm. A severe thunderstorm is known to render fish less active and thus less willing to cooperate with the waiting angler.

The sport fisherman, however, may wish to take advantage of this little-known storm warning. It is to be found in Charles C. Bombaugh's charming 1875 book, *Gleanings for the Curious from the Harvest-Fields of Literature: A Mélange of Excerpta*. Dr. Bombaugh has left us with:

For anglers in spring, it is always unlucky to see single magpies; but two may always be regarded as a favorable omen; and the reason is, that in cold and stormy weather one magpie alone leaves the nest in search of food, the other remaining sitting upon the nest or the young ones; but when two go out together it is only when the weather is warm and mild, and favorable for fishing.

THE FALSE

Unlike all that have gone before, the following predictions are not based on properly or improperly deciphered animal behaviors. Rather, they are superstitions that have evolved over the years. For example:

Step on an ant and it will rain.

Kill a daddy-longlegs spider and there's sure to be rain the next day.

Kill a beetle and it will rain.

All that can be said for the ant prediction is that were there a shred of truth to it, the world's umbrellas would be out and open every day of the week. The daddy-longlegs forecast seems obviously related to the bad luck promised on killing a spider, especially one with long legs.

Though quite as false as its companions, the beetle superstition has an interesting background. It may stem from the old British belief that the black beetle is a bad-luck insect. To see it anywhere in the house means future misfortune, and to have it scuttle over one's shoe or across someone who is lying down is a sign of death for the person himself or for someone close to him. Somewhere along the line the bad luck promised by the beetle was extended to include heavy rains. On the Isle of Man seven stormy days are promised for stepping on and killing a beetle.

An American superstition with an equally interesting background holds that if you

Bury a snake,
Good weather will make.
Hanging it high
Brings storm clouds nigh.

This old belief was especially widespread among the nation's slave population. Though completely without substance, it does have some logic to it. Like snails and frogs, snakes come out of their hiding places just before a rain, making their killing a commonplace at that time, an ugly job that often fell to the slaves. In those days the practice was to hang the dead snakes out to dry before disposing of them, and so it was easy to connect them with the arrival of the rain. The idea of burying the dead animals to fend off a storm is suspected of being a johnny-come-lately addition to the superstition. The snakes were probably first buried to be rid of the odor of their decay.

The practice of hanging dead snakes out to dry is an old one and was brought to the United States from a number of countries. It was much based on a belief in the efficacious powers of the animal's skin. For example, the people in certain parts of Britain believed—and some still do—that the dried skin, when nailed over the hearth, could bring good fortune to the family and protect the home from fire. And, for reasons that we'll see in the chapter on folk medicine, the snake and its skin have been admired through the ages for their healing powers. Among their admirers are those British and American rural folk who yet contend that rheumatism can be cured by wrapping a strip of the dried skin around the affected body part.

SEASONAL FORECASTS

The great bulk of predictions in this category deal with the coming of winter and the degree of its severity. To begin:

When squirrels collect a large store of nuts, you can expect the winter to be a severe one.

As logical as this forecast may seem at first glimpse, it is held to to be false, with naturalists explaining that squirrels are not blessed with an extrasensory perception when they lay in a richer-than-usual store of nuts. Rather they are are blessed with—and taking advantage of—a year that is producing an abundant food supply. Should the year provide a meager crop, the little animals would have to be content with whatever they could find, regardless of the mildness or severity of the winter.

Two more winter guesses that sound logical but are nevertheless false:

A bad winter is betide
If hair grows thick on the bear's hide.
—American Ozarks

When the buffalo hide is thick, the winter will be very cold.
—American Indian saying

Naturalists contend that thick coats on any furry animal have nothing to do with a sense of self-protection. Rather they indicate that the year has been a kind one. The animal has been given sufficient food to ensure the best of health, and the thickness of its coat reflects this. In addition, there is the argument that the animal's fur is thick not because the days are going to be cold but because they are already cold.

The same opinions hold for such similar animal forecasts as:

If turkey or chicken feathers are especially thick, look for a hard winter.

But there is a problem when we come to one of the most popular of winter predictions:

The wider the brown band on the woolly-bear caterpillar, the more severe the winter will be.

Certain as they may be about thick furry coats and plumage, naturalists don't know what to make of this one. The brown band is found midway along the caterpillar's body, with black stretching away to either side. Studies of the caterpillar have found that the prediction proves right more often than not. But no one can say whether there is a link between the size of the band and the severity of the coming winter or whether it's all a matter of coincidence.

There is no doubt, however, in the naturalist mind about the following two forecasts, both of which are New England favorites:

If the breastbone of your Thanksgiving turkey is light in color, the coming winter will bring heavy snows.

But:

If a goose is your main dish at Thanksgiving and its breastbone is of a darkish color, the winter will produce more rain than snow.

Both predictions are branded as false on the grounds that animal bones give no more indication of future weather than do animal furs.

Then there is this age-old European—and now American—superstition that gives us all some good fun every February 2:

When the groundhog comes out of his den to look at the weather, sees his shadow, and goes back inside, we will have six more weeks of winter.

The forecast is considered a harmless bit of nonsense by most naturalists. Their contention is that the groundhog or, in the American southwest, "Agua Fria Freddie," the sidewinder, retreats to his lair on a sunny February 2 not because he senses the continuation of winter but for quite another reason—a simple one of physical need. After long months underground, his eyes are painfully sensitive to sunlight. He scuttles back inside for relief.

They may be right. But were they to argue their case

before generations of European farm people, they would have little chance of being believed—this because February 2 is Candlemas Day, a religious holiday that dates back to Roman times, when candles were burned to drive away evil spirits. In the Christian era it was first called the Feast of the Purification of the Virgin Mary and later came to be known as the Presentation of Our Lord. Early on, European farmers began to use it as a gauge to measure the remaining length of winter. Out of what they saw of the weather that day came proverbs that are obviously the grandfathers of the groundhog prediction:

If Candlemas be fair and clear,
Two winters will you have this year.

Just as far as the sun shines in on Candlemas Day,
Just so far will the snow blow in before May.

A Welshman had rather see his dam on the bier
Than see a fair Februeer.

There was a good reason why the farmers disliked a "fair and clear" Candlemas Day. They looked on the first three months of the year as vital to a plentiful harvest of fruits, vegetables, and winter grains. The best harvests were promised when the winter moved gently along from January through March and produced a slow and steady thaw. A sudden warm spell brought on a premature thawing that was apt to be followed by a cold spell—the second of the "two winters will you have this year"—that would damage and perhaps kill the developing crops.

It was but a simple step from a dread of the sun on Candlemas Day to a fear of the animal shadows it created. In Europe, the bear and the badger became the chief harbingers of winter's duration. The early American farmer chose the groundhog, an animal whose February antics continue to charm us.

COLLECTIBLES

Horses

He who seeks a wife or a horse without fault has neither a steed in his stable nor an angel in his bed.

If you're riding a horse that suddenly bolts and runs away, you can stop him by biting his ear.

To ride (or go by) Shank's mare: To go somewhere on foot, with *shank* being a synonym for the leg. The saying is sometimes heard as *to ride* (or *go by) Shank's pony*. A British variation is *to ride the Marrow-bone stage*. It derives from a word play on the London district, Marylebone.

One foot white: buy him.
Two feet white: try him.
Three feet white: look well about him.
Four feet white: go without him.
                    —Old British advice on buying a horse

To flog (beat) a dead horse: To continue talking about a subject after your listeners have lost interest or to attempt to revive interest in a subject gone stale.

Put a beggar on horseback
And he'll ride to hell.

You can lead a horse to water, but you can't make him drink: The modern version of the following vintage proverbs on stubbornness and independence:

You may bring a horse to the river, but he will drink when and what he pleaseth.
　　　—George Herbert (1593–1632), *Jacula Prudentum*

A man may well bring a horse to the water, but he cannot make him drink without he will.
　　　　　　—John Heywood (1497–1580), *Proverbes*

Closing the barn door after the horse has bolted: A comment on actions taken too late.

God forbid that I should go to any heaven where there are no horses.
—Robert B. Cunninghame Graham (1852–1936), from a 1917 letter to Theodore Roosevelt

Every horse thinks its own load is the heaviest: an old British adage on self-pity.

A nod is as good as a wink to a blind horse: No matter how clever and good a hint or suggestion may be, it will be of no avail if the listener refuses or fails to heed it.

A horse, a wife, and a sword may be shewed but never lent.
　　　　　　　　　　　　　　—Ireland

A good horse sholde have three propyrtees of a man, three of a woman, three of a foxe, three of a hare, and three of an asse.
Of a man: Bolde, prowde, and hardye.
Of a woman: Fayre-breasted, faire of haire, and easy to move.
Of a foxe: a fair taylle, short eers, with a good trotte.
Of a hare: A grate eye, a dry head, and well rennynge (running).
Of an asse: A bygge chin, a flat legge, and a good hoof.
　　　　　　—Wynkyn de Worde (?–1534?),
　　　　　　British printer; Alsatian by birth

CHAPTER FIVE

Affairs of the Heart

IN WHAT WAS CERTAINLY a marriage of sheer imagination and everyday observation, our ancestors decided that certain animals were to play three roles in the affairs of the human heart. First, some were made to serve as sex and fertility symbols. Second, some were eaten as aphrodisiacs, those still-little-understood foods that are thought able to trigger sexual passion. And a third group occupied center stage in love rites and practices, often using the animals as omens of the future course of romance.

Echoes of these three tasks remain with us today. They can be detected in old superstitions still harbored across the world and in many of the expressions found in our daily speech. Who needs to be told, for instance, that an *old goat* is an aging, lecherous man?

THE SYMBOLS

Ranking high among the animals that seem to have meant the most to the ancients as sex and fertility symbols were the fish and the male goat. Of the two the fish was, for reasons we will see later, the far more admired. As for the goat, here's a look at what the ancients thought of the old boy.

The Goat

The goat early earned two contrasting reputations. On the one hand, he was respected for his stubbornness and agility, characteristics that made him a symbol of persistence and the ability to surmount obstacles. On the other, much because of his disgusting odor and insatiable appetite, he was early linked with evil and Satan. Out of that link came his connection with lechery and lust.

The link between the goat and evil can be seen in two tales—one Jewish, the other Egyptian—that stem from the ancient belief that wicked demons enjoyed mating with humans. The Old Testament book of Leviticus tells of the part played by goats in a Hebrew ritual performed on the Day of Atonement (Yom Kippur). Two goats were brought before the high priest, who then, by casting lots, designated one as the Lord's goat and the other as Azazel's. Azazel was the leader of those angels who had fallen from the heavenly heights because of their carnal dealings with earthly women. The Lord's goat was sacrificed, but Azazel's was ceremoniously burdened with the sins of the people, after which he was removed to the wilderness and allowed to escape, taking the sins with him.

It is from this ritual that we come by the term *scapegoat*, meaning someone on whom the blame is placed for the misdeeds of others. The word was originally *escapegoat*.

What may be more than a mere tale has it that in Egypt some five hundred years before Christ, the people of Mendes in the Nile delta worshiped a divine male goat. The practice was mentioned by the centuries-apart Greek historians Herodotus (485–425 B.C.) and Plutarch (ca. 46–120), with the latter reporting that the most beautiful women of the area were selected to lie with the goat divinity.

Both the Greeks and Romans saw the goat as something more than a symbol. They fashioned him into a deity—Pan in Greece and his Roman counterpart Faunus. Each was famous for his lechery, with Pan coming down to us as the better known of the two. He was the leader of the satyrs (fauns in Rome), rural spirits in whom human physical features were combined with those of the goat. Satyrs were depicted as having the bodies of humans and the horned heads, loins, legs and hooves of the goat. Lustful little creatures, they were constantly in the company of Dionysus (Bacchus to the Romans), the god of wine, and liked nothing better than frolicking at his orgiastic festivals. Their leader Pan was the patron of shepherds and goatherds. His godly function was to make the fields, woodlands, and flocks fertile.

(Satyrs are sometimes confused with their fellow rural spirits, centaurs. Centaurs were combinations of the human and the horse).

The Greeks envisioned Pan as a superb musician. He was especially adept at playing the reed pipe, the rustic instrument consisting of a series of graduated pipes, which emits a reedy sound when breath is blown across their upper ends. Always depicted with the pipe in hand, Pan is credited in myth with its invention. It seems that he got the idea for the instrument when he turned the woodland nymph Syrinx into a reed as she was fleeing his amorous advances.

Nymphs were female spirits of great beauty and charm, and the mention of Syrinx brings us to Pan's reputation for lechery and lust. He spent much of his time pursuing not only Syrinx but, apparently, every nymph within sight. The tales told about him have it that his efforts were usually successful.

As licentious as he was, there was something light and humorous (perhaps because of his association with the woodlands) about Pan. All traces of humor, however, had disappeared from any thoughts about the goat by the time of the Middle Ages. It was then that, more closely than ever before, he was linked to the idea of witchcraft. It was believed at that time that witches cohabited with the devil, who came to them in the form of a goat and sometimes a dog or monkey.

The Fish

To the ancient mind the fish represented many often-conflicting elements in life. In some cultures the fish stood for abundance, knowledge, wisdom, and women. In others it represented foolishness, stupidity, and greed. But there was one meaning on which a number of societies in widely separated regions were in agreement. For them, the fish represented fertility.

This meaning came principally from the fish's ability to lay a prodigious number of eggs. There was a sexual implication in its ability to swim through—to penetrate—the water (the ability to penetrate was also much responsible for association of the fish with knowledge). There was also a sexual implication in the similarity of the shape of certain species to the male sex organ.

The Egyptians, the Chinese, the Phoenicians, and the peoples of the neighboring states of how Assyria and Babylon all looked on the fish as a fertility symbol. The Egyptian view can be traced to the legend of the god of darkness, Set murdered his hated sun- and moon-god brother Osiris and then hacked his victim's body into fourteen pieces that he scattered throughout the countryside. Osiris's generative organ was thrown into the Nile River, where it was swallowed by a fish. Thereafter, the fish was associated with both gods. In connection with Osiris, it represented fecundity and rebirth. When linked with Set, it stood for evil, crime, and darkness.

Far across the world, the Carib Indians of the Caribbean and South America thought of the fish as always being young and believed that any man who lived on a fish diet would himself remain forever young, with, of course, his sexual powers intact. Thousands of miles to the north the natives of Greenland held that the eating of a certain fish could produce an astonishing result—pregnancy in both women and men.

In sharp contrast to its association with fertility, some societies considered the fish to be a symbol of sexual indifference. This idea remains with us today, in the expression a *cold fish*, which is used variously to mean a person of frosty nature or one of little sexual ardor. The latter was the more common meaning in bygone days and stemmed from the fact that certain fish are able to produce their young without mating.

The Greeks were not among those who looked on the fish as sexually indifferent. They found the fertility association so apt that they linked the animal to their love deities. One Greek legend has it that the love goddess Aphrodite was born in the sea from an egg brooded upon by a dove, after which she was shepherded to land by a fish. The range of love over which Aphrodite presided was so broad that she was known to her believers by two names—Aphrodite Pandemos, the goddess of all people (indicated by the root word *pan*) in matters of carnal and earthly love, and Aphrodite Urania, the goddess of the heavens and the patroness of pure love.

A number of European societies, while not associating the fish with their deities, did dream up that alluring nymph who is a combination of the human being and the fish—the mermaid. Customarily depicted as holding a mirror while combing her hair, she had the head and upper body of a beautiful woman and the lower body of a fish, complete with scales and tail. Her hair was long and is thought to have represented seaweed or the rays of the sun, while her mirror was envisioned as representing the moon disk.

In the folklore of such countries as Scotland and England, the mermaid was able to live on land. Though usually depicted as a shy creature who fled to the watery depths on seeing that she had been observed by a human, she apparently yearned for the pleasure of human company on occasion. Like her equally shy but less well-known counterpart, the merman, she especially liked to go ashore on market and fair days. For these forays the two would dress as peasants, a disguise that the watchful locals could easily penetrate. A corner of the mermaid's apron and the left side of the merman's coat were always wet.

Despite her shyness the mermaid's romantic dealings with humans were the subject of many European tales. There were stories of how she would fall in love with a man and entice him to live with her in the sea; stories of how, on falling in love with a man, she would assume a fully human shape and live ashore with him for a time, only to return for some reason to her watery realm; and stories of how she would take a human under her protection and then exact a terrible punishment on anyone who did him a wrong.

But legend, perhaps to show the dangers of love, also endowed the mermaid's nature with a dark side. Many stories told of human tragedy, especially death by drowning. There were stories of how she lured seamen to follow her beneath the waves and then led them to a watery kingdom from which there was no escape. Scandinavian legend has it that she could be seen dancing on the water just before a seaman drowned. In time the misfortune she threatened was extended from seafarers to all people.

The unhappy stories about the mermaid may have taken shape because she resembled the Sirens of Greek myth—those creatures who were half woman and half bird. Though mentioned by many Greek poets, they were immortalized by Homer (probably eighth century B.C.) in his *Odyssey*, where he described them as singing such sweet and seductive songs from their island home that they caused their listeners to forget all else and die of hunger. The Sirens came to represent any dangerously alluring woman.

Possibly the most famous of all such creatures is the Lorelei of Europe's Rhine River. According to this legend, a young maiden threw herself into the river in despair over a faithless lover. She then occupied a massive rock, called the Lorelei, near the right bank of the Rhine and sang seductive songs that lured sailors and fishermen to their deaths on the shoreline rocks and rapids. The men who glimpsed her lost their reason. Those who heard her song were doomed to remain with her forever. What seems to be at the base of the legend is the fact that the Lorelei rock is a place of odd echoes.

The mermaid, while similar to the Greek Siren, is widely thought to have come from Celtic legend. There is also the distinct possibility that both she and the Siren evolved from tales brought home by early sailing men of the dugong, a marine mammal whose female, commonly called a sea cow, resembles the human in two ways. Her head is roughly similar to that of the human head and she suckles her young by holding them to her breast, doing so by holding them in place with her flipper. The association with the Siren can be seen in the name that has been given to the aquatic order to which the dugong belongs—*Sirenia*.

THE APHRODISIACS

Of the animal foods that our forebears looked on as aphrodisiacs—those foods named for Aphrodite and thought able to stimulate sexually—oysters and certain fish were the most favored. But was there any sound scientific basis for this? Modern research into these foods, while not extensive, suggests that the answer is no. They do not contain sufficient quantities of substances (such as phosphorus) known to have an effect on the genito-urinary tract. Rather, two other factors are thought to have been responsible for arousal long ago. First, given the ability of fish to breed prolifically, it seems logical that the ancients would assume that the eating of the animal would transfer its sexual powers to them.

Second, and possibly of even greater significance to the ancients, were the distinct physical appearances of these fish and oyster. Not just these two foods, but others, such as asparagus and the vanilla plant, were thought to stimulate sexually because they resembled the human genitalia—the asparagus the penis, and the pod of the

vanilla plant the vagina; it is from the Spanish word for
the vagina—*vaina*—that the name of the plant is derived.
As for the fish, it resembled the penis. And the oyster?
Especially when on the half shell, it resembled the female's outer genitalia.

Among the fish foods that long ago joined oysters as
favored aphrodisiacs are eels, ocean shrimp, and the
freshwater crayfish. The eel was trusted because of its
obvious phallic shape. The renown of the shrimp owes
much to a short passage from the writings of Giovanni
Casanova (1725–1798), the Venetian author and sexual
adventurer. He wrote that he credited his sexual prowess
to a supper eaten by his mother on the eve of his birth;
the meal consisted of a bowl of spiced shrimp. As for
the crayfish, it had the reputation not only of arousing
passion but also of restoring the energy spent in sexual
activity.

The most dangerous of the animal foods thought to be
an aphrodisiac is Spanish fly, which is technically known
as *cantharides*. Concocted of beetles of the *cantharis
vesicatoria* species, Spanish fly is now recognized as
having a powerfully irritating effect on the genitourinary
tract, causing acute pain, difficulty in urinating, and
blood in the urine. As little as 1.5 grams of the substance
has been known to kill.

What has to be one of the oddest aphrodisiacs on record was reported in the 1849 book *Narrative of the Life
Adventures of Henry Bibb: An American Slave*. Bibb related how a witch doctor advised him that he could entice
any girl of his liking into his arms by scratching some
bare part of her body with the bone taken from a frog
and then dried. The promise was that the device would
work, no matter what the woman was doing at the time,
no matter with whom she was in love, and no matter
whether she was a stranger to Bibb or not. Bibb went on
to confess that when he tried this on a young lady pass-
erby, he won nothing from her but a shriek of pain and
an angry glare—undoubtedly because her assailant was a

stranger who struck without warning and, in his enthusiasm, dug a long furrow across her neck.

The bat is another odd—not to mention frightening—animal that once served as an aphrodisiac. There was a time in central Europe when a young girl, frustrated in matters of romance by a bashful or cool beau, would surreptitiously add a few drops of a bat's blood to her beloved's beer, all in the expectation of inflaming the fellow's desires and driving him into her arms.

Considering the bat's deplorable reputation in Europe, the practice seems not only odd but almost impossible to imagine. In great part because of its ugliness—and in greater part because it was able to fly and, even more significantly, fly in the dark—it was long the symbol of the demon who lives in darkness. European folklore linked it with the witch, ghost, and devilish imp. But as bad as it was in Europe, the bat's poor reputation was not shared worldwide. Both the Japanese and Chinese admired the creature. The Japanese called it *komori* and said it was symbolic of prosperity and happiness. To the Chinese, who called it *pien fu*, it was the bestower of good fortune and, because it supposedly lived for a thousand years, a long life. They also thought it a highly intelligent animal that was forced to hang with its head down because of the great weight of its brain. In the myths of some North American Indian tribes, it was depicted as a heroic creature dedicated to helping humans in distress.

And, in the midst of the fear shown it in Europe, there were those who considered the bat a lucky animal, among them the Hessians of Germany, who, remember, thought that good luck would come to the gambler who arrived for a card game with the creature's heart tied to his sleeve with a red string. The heart and the red string may be connected with the old idea that the bat's blood gave the animal its uncanny ability to fly in the dark. In turn, the idea that the bat's blood could bring luck at cards might have triggered the thought that the blood could bring a similar good fortune to romance.

The link between the bat and love was not limited to central Europe. Far across the world an aboriginal tribe in Australia's New South Wales regarded the bat as a symbol of love.

LOVE PRACTICES

The love practices in which animals played a part ranged from ancient rites aimed at ensuring or increasing individual or communal fertility to the myriad informal "rites" in which one could attempt to satisfy that age-old desire to glimpse the future—in this case, the future course of romance.

The Fertility Rites

Again, we begin with the goat. In Rome, during the annual fertility festival of Lupercalia, two young men with whips made of goatskin were sent dashing through the streets to lash out at the people they encountered. Any woman struck by the whips was deemed to be safe from barrenness. The festival, which featured sacrifices of goats and dogs to Faunus (Rome's equivalent of Pan), was intended to ensure not only the fertility of the people but also that of their crops and fields. It was held each February at the Lupercal, the spot where the legendary founders of the city, the twins Romulus and Remus, had been abandoned and where they were suckled by a she-wolf after their mother, the vestal virgin Rhea Silvia, was condemned to death for conceiving them.

The fish, being the worldwide symbol of fertility that it was, inspired a variety of odd practices. For one, the people of medieval Europe often burned rather than ate fish during their fertility rites. The idea here was that the odor of the burning fish would drive off the evil spirits hostile to love and procreation. The strategy was an ancient one by medieval times and may have stemmed from an incident reported in the Apocrypha's Book of Tobit, written, you'll recall, some two centuries before Christ. The incident concerns a burning fish that drove away a spirit that interfered with love.

In the South Pacific the husband of a childless wife was told to travel to the "Childless Sea" on the coast of Java, take a fish from its waters, and eat it. Then he would be able to beget offspring.

Virgins in such widely separated locales as Samoa, India, and Brazil were given fish as gifts with the assurance that the gifts would induce pregnancy. The practice continues to this day, and there are stories of the women having actually been fertilized by the gifts.

The dog, the mole, and the marmot have also won a reputation as fertility foods. An old American superstition, said to be inherited from Europe, holds that the eating of cooked dog meat will help a sterile woman to become fertile. In parts of France the blood of the mole—an animal that, as we will see in the upcoming chapter on medicine, was highly regarded throughout the ancient world for its alleged healing properties—was recommended as a drink for the man who wished to regain his virility.

The role of the marmot, especially in rural areas of Switzerland, was to help the fertile woman remain fertile after giving birth. Soon after delivery, she was to eat the little rodent's fat on the theory that the animal's talent for breeding many healthy and (if the way in which they cavort about is any indication) happy offspring would be passed on to her.

And we must not forget that traditional symbol of fertility, the egg. In France, the bride of the seventeenth century ate an egg on entering her new home to ensure that her marriage would be a bountiful one. Moroccan males who wish to improve their sexual potency and capacity have long observed the rite of eating an egg yolk at the start of each morning for forty days.

But what about the other side of the coin? What of the

desire not to procreate? The ancient world—like the modern—had its folk versions of the pill. For the Romans the marrow from an eagle bone was thought to serve as a contraceptive. In regions of India today, the woman who wishes to avoid pregnancy believes that she can do so by catching a frog, spitting in its face three times, and then leaving the animal where she found it.

Omens of Future Romance

American folklore, especially in New England and the southern and southwestern regions of the nation, abounds with superstitious practices that rely on the animal as an omen of love's future course. In common with the myriad practices involving good or bad luck, most are centuries-old European transplants that initially took shape through the concidental sighting of an animal and some subsequent occurrence. What else can be said of the beliefs that marriage will come quickly to the girl who stumbles over a dog or a cat, has a bee fly near her head, finds one in her shoe, has a butterfly flit close by, steps on a cat's tail, or glimpses a bird after dark?

By far the greatest number of the practices concern the future of young women, with birds—especially the red-bird, bluebird, and that age-old symbol of peace, the dove—playing major roles as the diviners of love. For example, on hearing the call of the first doves returning in springtime, a young girl of rural America is supposed to walk a few steps and then look inside her right shoe, there to find a hair that matches the hair color of the man she will marry. The custom was likely brought here from England, where young girls did the same thing on hearing the season's first cuckoo.

In a variation of the practice the girl who hears the coo of a dove is to keep her eye out for the next man who rides by. He will be her future husband.

The dove's association with romance as well as peace probably stems in part from a tale told of Aphrodite and her son, Eros. As the story goes, the two were engaging in a game of picking flowers. Aphrodite was winning because she was being assisted by a nymph named Peristera. A frustrated Eros turned the nymph into a dove. Thereafter, the gentle bird enjoyed the protection of Aphrodite.

What of the redbird or bluebird? When one or the other flies in the path of a girl, it means that she will soon be kissed by a true love.

The redbird is also an omen of another kind of romantic good fortune: when glimpsed by either a boy or a girl, it promises that a love letter is on the way and will soon arrive.

Still another redbird superstition: whenever you see a redbird, be sure to throw three kisses at it before it flies out of sight. Then you will have good luck, either in romance or some other area of your life.

Even the unattractive crow has won a place as an omen. Should you see a number of crows flying overhead, be sure to count them. If they number four, there's a birth in your future. A count of three means that a wedding (perhaps yours) is in the offing. Two mean mirth. But watch out for just one. It foretells sorrow.

Also, if you are an expectant mother who was reared on the folklore of Utah, the sight of three single crows flying in the same direction on the same day will not please you. It means that your child will grow up to be a vagabond.

That purveyor of all types of luck, the horseshoe, also plays a special role in matters of the heart. If a girl places the shoe over the doorway of her home just before dawn on May 1 and then keeps close watch on the door, she will soon see someone who resembles the man destined to be her husband. That someone will be the first person to pass through the door.

The superstition may stem from the aura of romance that has always surrounded the ancient May Day springtime festival, which is still widely observed on May 1, sharing the date with Labor Day in some countries. In

Rome, young people spent the festival in the fields, dancing and singing in honor of Flora, the goddess of flowers and fruits. The British of old set up a maypole for dancing, engaged in various sports, and paid homage to the legendary Robin Hood and his love, Maid Marian, as the lord and lady of the festivities.

It is possible that the horseshoe superstition gave birth to two similar backwoods practices, one involving the lucky four-leaf clover, the other the cabbage stump. In the first a young woman pins the clover above her door; the first unmarried man who then passes beneath is the one she is destined to marry. In the second a young man or woman takes a moment on Halloween to do the same thing with the cabbage stump; the first member of the opposite sex to come through the door will be his or her future spouse.

The glimpse of a number of animals gives us the opportunity to make a wish. The wish can be for any kind of good fortune, but because it will concern a matter of love, let's spend a moment with these charmed animals now. Be sure to make a wish when you:

See a swarm of bees.

Hear the first frogs of spring.

Catch sight of two piebald horses in succession.

See several white horses.

Hear the first robin of spring.

Your wish, however, will not come true unless you take care to observe some time-honored traditions. First and foremost, in all the above cases (and in every other wish-making instance, such as blowing out birthday candles, tossing a coin into a wishing well, or winning a "wishbone pull" contest), you must never mention your wish to anyone; the slightest mention—even a slip of the tongue—instantly cancels out all the magic. Next, should the piebald horses amble past, one after another, be sure that you spit three times and count up to ten after making your wish. Finally, should you run across a collection of white horses, remember that your wish will come to naught unless you delay making it until you count the horses up to three and then shake hands with someone.

A variation of the white-horse belief calls for a girl to keep track of the white horses she sees. When her count reaches ninety-nine, she can be assured that she will one day be standing at the altar with the next man who shakes her hand or tips his hat to her.

For the most part the omens of future romance promise a happy outcome. But there are those that bespeak of misfortune, and the egg, that symbol of fertility, is one of them. Some young women still follow the unappetizing Irish and Scottish custom of removing the yolk from an egg and filling the hole with salt, after which they eat the egg and shell. The concoction is to be downed at midnight, with the girl then being forbidden to drink water until the morning. Should she dream that her lover is bringing her water, it means that he will soon discard her for another.

The cat and the mule are also widely considered harbingers of romantic misfortune—that is, for any young woman who considers the single state unfortunate. For her, we close with these backwoods warnings:

If you like cats better than dogs, you'll not marry.

Never ride a mule. If you do, you'll end up an old maid.

Forest and Jungle Creatures

The wolf may lose his teeth but never his nature.

You've seen the wolf: You've seen something that has greatly frightened you. Originally, the saying was addressed to someone who had lost his voice and was based on the old peasant superstition that a person, on glimpsing a wolf, was left without speech for a time.

Busy as a beaver.

The Badger State: Wisconsin.

Like a bear sucking his paws: Not often heard today, this saying refers to someone who is "working hard" at being idle. It comes from the old fancy that the bear, when without food, could keep himself alive by sucking nourishment from his paws.

The little foxes, that spoil the vines.

—Song of Solomon

Should you see a squirrel on your way to school, be sure to watch which way it runs. If it scoots off to your right, you will learn your lessons well that day. But if it runs to your left, you will miss your lessons.

—A child's superstition

Keep the wolf from the door.

Quick like a bunny: Great speed, sometimes in sexual matters. A mild bit of vulgarity, the saying refers to the rapidity with which rabbits breed.

To badger someone: To annoy, tease, or pester a person to an extreme. The phrase grew out of the old and cruel sport of badger baiting. The animal was placed in a tub or a box and dogs were loosed to drag him back out, after which the victim was allowed to rest a few moments before being returned to his prison for a repeat of the "game."

Three traits of the fox: a light step, a look to the front, and a glance to each side of the road.

—Ireland

The hare always returns to her form: A comment on the joys and value of staying at home.

How much wood would a woodchuck chuck if a woodchuck could chuck wood? A woodchuck would chuck all that a woodchuck would chuck if a woodchuck could chuck wood.

—A child's tongue twister

And, finally, from the rain forests and jungles:

Darwinian Man, though well behaved,
At best is only a monkey shaved.
  —William S. Gilbert (1836–1911), *Princess Ida*

Or as Charles Darwin (1809–1882) himself put it:

The Simiadae then branched off into two great stems, the New World and the Old World monkeys; and from the latter at a remote period, Man, the wonder and the glory of the universe, proceeded.

—*The Descent of Man*

Monkey see, monkey do.

CHAPTER SIX

To Your Health

ANIMALS HAVE PLAYED a variety of significant roles in the history of medicine. For one, when the dissection of human cadavers was forbidden several centuries ago as a desecration of God's handiwork, scientists depended on animal vivisection to fathom the inner workings of the body, doing so on the quite sensible premise that animal and human organs functioned in much the same manner. For another, it was with microbes taken from diseased animals that the world's first vaccines were created to combat such global killers as smallpox and tuberculosis. In modern medicine animals continue to be the subjects of laboratory research into human diseases and disorders.

But these functions all have to do with medicine as a science. What assistance did animals give the art of healing that can be placed within the context of folklore? Here, they took on two assignments. First, they served the physician in medical procedures and as ingredients in medications at a time when there was no such thing as a pharmacy. Second, they served generations of people as the basis for home remedies.

THE ANIMAL AND THE ANCIENT PHYSICIAN

The role of the animal in healing dates back to the very beginnings of medical history. No better proof of this is needed than a painting high on a wall in the French cave

112

called *Les Trois Frères*, the Cave of the Three Brothers. On view there is the painted figure of a strange manlike creature with animals prancing about him. The figure and the lunging beasts are estimated to have been the work of an artist living sometime between seventeen thousand and twenty-five thousand years ago.

The creature is an awesome sight. His head is decorated with the antlers of a stag. He wears the skin of an animal, possibly that of a bear or bison. He has the tail of a horse, the paws of a bear, and ears similar to those of a wolf. He seems to be dancing, his body leaning forward, his feet lifted, and his arms extended. While some scholars conjecture that he might have been the depiction of a god, others believe that he is a representation of one of the world's first doctors. They call him the "Sorcerer" and look on him as the ancestor of all medical men.

If the Sorcerer indeed represents a physician, it is his costume—everything from his antlered headdress to his bear-paw gloves—that is of significance to our story. It is significant because it is clearly tied to two of the several elements on which the world's earliest medicine was based. First, there was the belief that illness was the work of invisible demons that invaded the body; such creatures lurked everywhere—in the air, on rooftops, in the corners of a room—and were ready to pounce on anyone at any time, while others were the agents of the gods sent to punish an individual for some transgression. Second, there was the deep fear that wild animals triggered in ancient man.

In light of these two elements, there can be little doubt about how the earliest of medical reasoning must have run: if animals can strike terror in the human heart, then they must also have the power to drive off the demons of illness. What better way for a physician (or, as he was variously called, priest, shaman, witch doctor) to get results than to rig himself up as some terrible beast and then descend, prancing and shouting, on his patient?

Would not a demon with any sense of self-preservation whatsoever depart the patient and flee for its life?

There was another reason for the costume, one that was likewise based on a deep-seated fear of and respect for the animal. It had to do with a point made several times in this book. Many cultures revered the animal as a god or a sacred spirit because they thought it was endowed with magical, supernatural powers. In North America the Iroquois Indians held that the bear spirit caused spasms and the buffalo spirit rheumatism. Deep in the Pacific the Tahitians worshiped the hermit crab and said that if one were eaten without appropriate rites, death would follow. So why shouldn't the Sorcerer and his kind have donned a costume—whether it be made of furs or feathers—to arm themselves with those selfsame magical powers?

The psychological effect of the costume must not be overlooked. To gain the trust of their patients—perennially acknowledged as vital in medical care—doctors throughout the ages have identified themselves by their professional dress, from the Sorcerer's animal garb to the flowing robes and conical hat of the Sumerian physician and on to the white smock of the modern practioner.

Magic Medicines

But the early doctor did not depend on his costume alone to overcome the demons of illness. From the Sorcerer onward, he devised animal medicines (and those from trees, plants, and bushes) thought to contain magical properties that could send the demons fleeing. These medicines were of two basic types. There were, first, those that helped patients put up a better fight by transferring to them animal strengths and supposed curative powers. Then there were the medicines that got their magic from the disgusting ingredients that went into them. Working by themselves or in tandem with the doctor's costume, they had the power to drive the demons off. Consider these examples of the first type:

Some societies cloaked their patients in animal skins for the purpose of transmitting to them the animal strength and ferocity needed to combat a deadly illness. It was a practice that is still found today among certain primitive tribes.

It was common in a number of widely separated regions for children to be fed animal parts to endow them with characteristics needed for both health and survival: for instance, the lion's heart, the jaguar's tail, and the eagle's wings for strength and courage, and the chameleon's eyes for slyness. Conversely, a number of peoples refused to eat the tortoise for fear it would cost them their fleetness of foot. Again, we have here practices that are still followed today in some parts of the world.

To rid a patient of cataracts, the Romans devised a poultice that consisted of the liver of an eagle mixed with balsam and honey. It was applied on the theory that since the eagle was blessed with magnificent eyesight, its liver—gorged as it was with that vital life-giving substance, blood—could alleviate vision problems. In nearby Greece the liver was thought to be the seat of passion.

The Egyptians treated one of the most common complaints heard in their dry and dusty land, inflamed and sore eyes, with a paste made of the gall of a frog because they thought the little animal carried some magical curative property. The concoction was of no genuine therapeutic value, but may have done some psychological good because of its alleged hidden powers. What actually helped was the treatment that preceded its application. The patient downed a drink of beer and onions, which relieved the eyes by making them water, after which they were bathed with soothing ointments.

The animal and magic were combined in a number of ancient procedures as well as medications. Various North American Indian tribes performed healing dances in which the participants imitated such animals as the bear and the buffalo spirits. Some of the dances were performed by the tribal doctor. The entire community joined in others.

One of the most interesting medical procedures was to be seen more than six thousand years ago. Aeons before scientific diagnosis and prognosis were commonplace, the physicians of Sumer, one of the sun-drenched lands lying between the Tigris and Euphrates rivers, attempted to chart the future course of illnesses by means of hepatoscopy—the study, you'll recall from an earlier chapter, of an animal's liver. The animal—usually a sheep, a goat, or a chicken—was first sacrificed by the patient's family, after which its body was opened and the liver examined to see what it prophesied. The liver was used for the same reason it was employed in the Roman poultice—because it was gorged with blood. If the organ proved to be malformed in any way, a long illness lay ahead for the patient. If a blood vessel ran in one direction, recovery was promised; if it traveled in another direction, death could result. Should a tumor be found in the organ, death was a certainty.

Doctors in ancient China employed animal bones in a similar procedure. Into the surface of what he called an Oracle Bone, a physician would scratch a question about a patient's health. Then he would hold the bone over a fire until the flames cracked its surface. The answer to the question was to be seen in the various patterns etched by the heat.

Archaeological diggings have unearthed Oracle Bones throughout China. They have been found to be covered with questions not only about health but about other aspects of life as well. Nor have the scratchings been limited to questions alone. Some bones are incised with descriptions of diseases that, though not given names recognizable to us, match such familiar ailments as tuberculosis, typhoid fever, malaria, and leprosy.

On turning to the medicines meant to disgust the demons of illness into flight, we come to concoctions made up of such ingredients as sulfur, plant roots, human excrement, and animal entrails, hair, skin, bones, and dung. The patient was forced to swallow a stinking, vile-tasting stuff or to lie still while it was drained into his ear, thrust up his nose, or smeared over his body and massaged into his pores (all this on the theory that the demons entered the body via its various openings). Sometimes it stench was such that it only had to be waved close to him. The hoped-for result was that the foul taste, smell, or very look of the medication, helped along with prayers, incantations, and the pounding of drums, would send the demons scuttling out of the body.

At work here in tandem with the magic was a human belief that, in all the centuries since, has never really gone away—the odd and perhaps masochistically or sadistically inspired conviction that the worse a medicine tastes or looks, the more effective it is certain to be. The trust that humans have placed in loathsome medicines can be seen throughout the course of medical history. To find the animal in many such medications, we need only look at the following examples from widely spaced eras in that history:

The eminent Greek physician Pliny the Elder, in his *Natural Science*, wrote that the bite of a scorpion could be cured by roasting and eating "the same scorpion that did the harm" and then drinking two glasses of wine. He also advised that the scorpion be placed on the wound it had made.

A fellow Greek of even greater eminence, Galen (130–200), whose scientific writings and astute observations influenced European medicine through the Renaissance, once advised that toothache could be cured by holding a frog that had been boiled in water and vinegar in the mouth.

European doctors between the sixteenth and nineteenth centuries treated a wide variety of ills with an evil-tasting, poisonous salt because of an odd circumstance involving pigs. The salt, known at the time as *stibium*, became popular when the alchemist Paracelsus (1493–1541) wrote of how he had seen some pigs grow fat after eating the substance. Fancying himself a doctor (he had no medical training whatsoever), Paracelsus decided to see if it would likewise help several monks who had dwindled to mere shadows of themselves due to extended fasting. The fact that all his patients died (causing the stuff to be renamed *antimony*, meaning "antimonk") failed to stop generations of medicos from administering it.

In early American history the preacher and self-appointed physician Cotton Mather (1663–1728) devised an abominable remedy for helping newborns overcome the "Effects of Sins" bequeathed to them by the folly of Adam and Eve. Though sharing a lack of medical training with Paracelsus, he nevertheless took it upon himself to write that parents were to deposit a half pound of live sowbugs in a quart or two of wine, then to feed their infants the concoction twice a day at the rate of two ounces per feeding. (The Reverend Mather was never a man much loved for his compassionate ways.)

As if the medicines were not bad enough, they were joined by procedures quite as upsetting. Leeches were used worldwide for centuries to bleed fever patients, on the theory that fever was a heating of the blood (or, earlier, the result of the invasion of demons) and could be eased by reducing the amount of blood in the body. They were also applied to those bruised results of so many tavern and street melees: black eyes. Bloodletting, which is known to have begun in prehistoric times and was initially practiced with knives to wash the demons of illness away, finally went out of style in Europe and the United States (where George Washington was once so treated) in the latter half of the nineteenth century. It is still employed in Mexico, South America, the Orient, and a few U.S. backwoods areas. The practice is thought to have saddled the doctor of yesteryear with the disrespectful nickname that is still heard, though rarely, today: *leech*.

Actually, the reverse is true. It is the leech that received its name from the doctor. The word is derived from the Old English word *laece*, meaning "a healer" or "one who relieves pain," and was early applied to British physicians, with the practice of medicine itself being known as *leechcraft*. The animal was later given the name because of its supposed healing powers. Today, the slang word *leech* usually refers to someone of a parasitical nature.

Not All Magic

All this is not meant to say that the medicine of old was without its scientific side. Much rational thinking was on view among the ancients in the midst of their magical practices and potions. It is recognized today, for example, that the bear, buffalo, and other healing dances of the North American Indians were of genuine medical value both physiologically and psychologically— physiologically because they involved the ingestion of health-giving herbs and plants by the patient, and psychologically because of their calming effect on patients mentally upset by their illnesses or suffering from mental disorders.

The Egyptians and Sumerians were just two of the many peoples whose physicians joined the North American tribes in recognizing the curative properties of plant, herbal, and animal products. They early developed medicines containing milk and honey (both of which symbolized immortality in several cultures), yeast, mineral oils, figs, dates, and, to reduce pain and tension, opium. Though it was the tradition to mix these ingredients with the likes of animal entrails and excrement for magical effect, the doctors at times sensibly and compassionately departed from the norm and mixed them with beer to make them palatable. But quite often there was a mystical reason for the departure. When a demon refused to flee from some medicinal abomination, the strategy was to coax him out with something of pleasant taste and aroma.

Not at all mystical, however, was the use to which black ants were put in an ancient surgery. Both the African witch doctor and the physician in India sutured wounds with their aid. The ants, on being placed along the length of a wound, bit into the surrounding flesh, at which time the surgeon snapped off their bodies, leaving their heads and clamped jaws behind as stitches. The Indian doctors, employing giant black Bengali ants, applied the technique to internal as well as external wounds, particularly those of the intestines. The fomic acid in the ants held a bonus for the patient: it served as an antiseptic that helped to safeguard against infection.

Nor was there anything mystical in a number of animal medicines that emerged through the centuries. The physicians of old, for instance, did not know the scientific reasons why boiled toads helped in cases of dropsy or why burned sponges aided goiter patients. But they knew something more important from experience. They knew that these odd medications worked. Modern science has taught us that toad skins contain diuretic alkaloids and that sponges contain iodine.

Though the ancients were wide of the mark in putting the blame on demons, they were pretty much on target in sensing a basic cause of much disease. They knew nothing of the microbe and what it can do to the body, but their belief in demons leaves no doubt of their understanding that much sickness is generated by an outside agency—something in the air, in a friend's breath or touch, in a sick person, his bedding, and his belongings.

That something came through the air and was caught and taken into one's body. The Romans invented a word for epilepsy that meant "to be caught" or "seized." We of the twentieth century speak as the ancients did when we talk of catching a cold or refer to an epileptic attack as a seizure.

The ancients, though unable to identify what it was, also knew there was something evil in certain foods and forbade their use. Possibly the best known of the bans was that which the early Jews placed on the eating of pork. That they had a point in calling pork an "unclean food" was established centuries later when science discovered the microbial *trichinella* parasites coiled in cysts in the muscles of pigs. They give the name *trichinosis* to the illness that can come of eating underdone pork.

Somewhere at the back of the ancient mind there must have been some vision, however blurred, of the microbe itself. Several cultures depicted their demons of illness as tiny animals. The Babylonians and Assyrians believed that toothache was caused by a gnawing worm (an idea that persisted in Europe until well into the eighteenth century). The Sumerian god of death and pestilence, Nergal, was often represented as a tiny insect (he was also pictured as a winged creature with the head of a man and the body of a lion).

The Chinese vision of the microbe seems to have been less cloudy. For perhaps more than a century before Britisher Edward Jenner developed the world's first smallpox vaccine, Chinese doctors were protecting their patients against the disease with a powder in which the fleas removed from cows infected with cowpox (smallpox in cattle) were mixed. The powder, which the patient inhaled, worked in the same way as all the vaccines to come: it gave the patient a mild case of a disease that rendered him immune. (Actually, the Chinese had been combating smallpox since 1050 with powders made of the scabs lifted from the pocks that cover the smallpox victim's body. The disease was introduced into China by barbarian invaders in about the year 50.)

The idea of immunity was the inspiration for a major pre-Christian pharmacological investigation whose echoes could still be heard early in our own century. Its roots extended back to studies that virtually all the ancient societies conducted for the purpose of developing poisons from animals, especially from the venomous asp, viper, and water snake. Sought were toxins that could be of immediate use in arrows and that might also have a medicinal value. One such research effort—pursued in Egypt—caught the eye of visiting Greek physicians, who then passed the news on to Mithridates VI (132–63 B.C.), the king of Pontus, a realm on the Black Sea.

An ardent pharmacologist as well as a sovereign, Mithridates embarked on an investigation to determine if a venomous serpent could be used not as a poison but as an antidote against all types of poisoning. His plan was based on the knowledge that, though the snake could kill its victim, it was immune to its own bite. This being the case, Mithridates reasoned that the meat of the snake or some form of its venom might well provide a human with the same immunity.

The king's study resulted in a medication named *mithridaticum* in his honor. Though composed of as many as sixty-three substances in its assorted recipes, the main ingredient was the flesh of the viper. Sometime later, the formula was altered by physicians and the concoction was rechristened *theriac*, becoming a medicine that was to serve generations of Europeans and then Americans as a general cure-all. "Snake oils" were foisted on the European and American publics by medicine-show quacks and physicians as elixirs able to cure anything from rheumatism to middle-age fatigue.

At some point in its history *theriac* underwent another change of name—this time to treacle. When the medicine was eventually discarded because, like *mithridaticum*, it was finally judged medically worthless, the new name lingered on and came to mean molasses. Until just a few years ago, an unappealing mixture of sulfur and treacle was routinely administered to all youngsters as a spring tonic.

The serpent's association with medicine, however, is not limited to the poison studies that led to treacle. The animal has come down to us from antiquity in the symbol of the medical profession, the snake-entwined caduceus—a symbol thought strange by many because it links an animal widely regarded as deadly with a calling dedicated to the preservation of life.

The Caduceus

Symbolically, the serpent was both hated and loved among the ancients. It was widely seen by some societies as symbolizing death, deceit, treachery, revenge, pleasure and lasciviousness (perhaps stemming from its use as a phallic symbol), cunning, malice, and—due to its nefarious ways in the Garden of Eden—temptation. But in sharp contrast, other cultures looked on it as representing such positive life forces as intelligence, wisdom, and healing.

This dual outlook was especially seen among the Greeks. While their mythology spoke of such evil creatures as the Medusa with her hair of writhing snakes, they also saw a positive connection between the serpent and renovation. Responsible for the link was the animal's ability to shed its skin without dying or, as the Greeks put it, his ability to dispense with his old age and return to his youth to start life again. To them it was a characteristic obviously analogous to the medical healing that enables the patient to "shed" his illness and begin life anew.

The Greeks' admiration of the snake survived long after their civilization's decline. It was echoed in Renaissance times by British dramatists Francis Beaumont (1584–1616) and John Fletcher (1579–1625) when they had one of their characters remark:

You have eat a snake
And are grown young, gamesome and rampant.

In Greek legend the snake's alleged curative powers made it sacred to Apollo, the god of the sun and music. The snake was also associated with Hermes, the messenger of the gods (better known to us by his Roman counterpart, Mercury). Hermes was envisioned as a young man whose winged hat and ankles enabled him to travel everywhere with the speed of the wind. Held in his hand was the caduceus, the snake-entwined rod that even then had a medical connotation because it enabled him to bring sleep to anyone he wished. Variously seen today as a winged staff girdled by two snakes or an unadorned staff with a single snake, the caduceus became a definite medical fixture when Hermes presented it to Aesculapius, the god of healing. Aesculapius later found a place in Roman legend when, in the form of a snake, he was introduced into Rome during a time of pestilence around 300 B.C.

It is widely thought that the caduceus originated in Egypt, perhaps a result of studies of venomous snakes, and that it was brought to the Greeks by their early physicians who had visited the Nile regions. From Greece and then Rome it made its way to our own time.

FOLK MEDICINE

The world has produced literally thousands of folk remedies for everything from the most serious of illnesses to the general malaise that we describe as the "blahs." Some remedies, initially devised by physicians, remained among the common people long after going out of style or being branded as useless by science. Some were concocted by the unlicensed practioners—the witch doctors, conjurers, healers, magicians, and voodoo priests—who hung out their shingles on every continent. Some were invented by the people themselves in the absence of trained medical personnel.

Used in all these remedies was everything that nature had to offer—plants, herbs, water, minerals, even human urine (long advised for the young woman who desired a lovely complexion was a daily morning massage with her own urine). And, of course, the animals, from the largest to the smallest, were summoned.

Of Snakes, Eels, and Unicorns

Let's begin with the larger animals. If you travel to Kentucky, you'll find that you can prevent headaches by wearing a headband fashioned of the rattles of the rattlesnake. In Kentucky and elsewhere you can ease a rheumatic pain by rubbing the affected area with the snake's skin (the British do the same thing with the skin of an adder). To the south, in Louisiana, rheumatic pain can be alleviated with a coating of grease from either the rattlesnake or the alligator. And you'll be able to protect yourself against warts and a variety of illnesses by wearing a bag containing alligator teeth.

In various parts of the nation—New England among them—you'll find that an eelskin wrapped around the midsection will hold rheumatism at bay; for stomachache or cramps, wrap the eelskin around your ankle. A cat's tail, if rubbed gently against the eyelid, will make a sty go away. If your child has fits, you're to give the youngster a puppy. The child is to play and sleep with the dog so the youngster's problem will be transmitted to the animal. The child's condition will improve as the animal's worsens, with the cure being complete at the time the puppy dies.

On journeying to Europe you'll hear tales of how, in the Middle Ages, the stag was considered the healthiest of all animals, one that was believed immune to the fevers of the time. To ward off a fever attack, you had only to mix the powdered marrow of the stag's horn in a mug of ale or hot wine. You had to take care, however, to use the marrow from the right horn, which was said to be the most powerful part of the stag and was thus able to provide the greatest protection.

Speaking of horns, let us not forget the powers that Europeans attributed to the fabled unicorn horn. It was so valued for its supposed abilities to detect and neutralize poison that it was treasured by royal families—always in danger of poisoning by court enemies—throughout continental Europe and in England. It was so treasured, in fact, that purchasing it was far beyond the reach of the common people. In his book *Devils, Drugs and Doctors* Howard W. Haggard reports that in sixteenth-century Germany a specimen of the stuff sold for the 1970s' equivalent of $75,000.

The unicorn itself was a mythical animal that was said to have the head and body of a horse, the legs of a buck, and the tail of a lion. Thrusting up from its forehead was a single horn that was red at the tip, black at the center, and white at the base. The horn was so highly prized because medieval legend credited the animal with being able to dip it into a liquid and immediately detect and counteract any poison that might be there. Actually, what was sold as unicorn horn was simply ivory and is thought to have been obtained from the narwhal.

(The rhinoceros horn enjoyed a popularity in the Orient equal to that of the unicorn horn in Europe—and for the same reason: its supposed ability to detect the presence of poison in liquids. A liquid, on being poured into the horn, was said to begin frothing immediately. The Chinese also credited the horn with medicinal and aphrodisiac properties. The unceasing demand for it as an aphrodisiac has long caused the rhinoceros to be relentlessly hunted and is said to be in great part responsible for the animal's status today as an endangered species. Prized as it is, the horn has always carried an enviable price tag. In the seventeenth century its exorbitant cost led to the use of *rhino* as a Western slang term for money.)

Linger in certain areas of France and you'll find the pig much respected; the country folk there are convinced that a slice of boiled ham (accompanied by a glass of wine) at bedtime will take care of such matters as flu, gout, dizziness, coughing, and the "blahs." A French cure that was transplanted to Canada calls for a piece of fresh pork to be rubbed on unwanted hairs, after which, accompanied by a prayer demanding the hairs to depart, it is buried and left to rot in the ground.

Of Roaches, Moles, and Toads

To see the smaller animals at work, let's begin our travels again in the United States. Visit the French in Louisiana and you'll find that a juice in which roaches are mixed will serve you well as a cure for colds and sore throats, that a drink laced with boiled lizard tails also does well with colds and with colic and fevers, and that the application of a spiderweb is advised to cure cankers and put a stop to bleeding. Elsewhere in the south and in other parts of the country, you'll learn that one of the best cures for whooping cough is a soup made of nine frogs. Should you, on venturing into New England, happen to drink too much one night, you'll find that your best bet for ridding yourself of a hangover is to eat two pounds of honey and settle down for twenty-four hours of rest.

On crossing the Atlantic, you'll come upon those in England who still believe that the death of a terminally ill patient can be delayed by placing a dove in his or her room, the purpose being to keep the patient alive until friends and loved ones can arrive for a final farewell. The strategy, which is based on the old concept that the dove symbolizes not only peace but also the soul, seems to be that the soul enjoys the bird's company so much that it will delay its departure from the sickroom.

No matter where you wander in Europe, you are apt to hear about folk cures involving the lowly, burrowing mole. Though despised in many ancient cultures because it lived underground, in what was thought to be the realm of the dead, the little animal was much respected by the Persians, the Greeks, and the Romans. Their respect was based on its ability to survive within the earth—to survive despite the fact that it was assumed to be blind. Out of this respect came the belief that its strengths could be passed into the sick to make them well again. In time, the mole's reputation spread from the Mediterranean regions to all of Europe. Its use as a folk medication in Europe persisted until well into this century and continues to be practiced by some rural peoples.

Many of the mole cures demanded that the animal be sacrificed, after which its blood or flesh was rubbed into or fed to the patient. There was a widespread belief that drinking of the animal's blood cured epilepsy and drunkenness. The French poured it into the ear to end deafness; both the French and English massaged it into the skin to erase wens and warts; the Czechoslovakians smeared it on the body to cure scrofula. The people in a number of regions applied the animal's viscera to rheumatic areas of the body.

The mole also served as an amulet. A French mother often made a necklace of a string dipped in the animal's blood and placed it around her infant's neck to prevent bed-wetting. It was common practice throughout Europe to wear the animal's paw as a safeguard against epilepsy, a tradition that later found a place in American folk medicine. It was also common practice to wear a small sack containing the paws as a protection against toothache and rheumatism.

For centuries, the mole was not only used as a medication or an amulet but also considered the source from which doctors and healers obtained their power to cure. The animal's efficacy was transmitted to them in rituals in which they held him in the hand for a length of time, cut or ripped him apart, or impaled him on a finger. They were then able to cure illnesses and disorders ranging from wounds, fevers, and deadly cancers to boils and other body sores.

As closely linked as the mole to the folk medicine of both Europe and the United States is that small relative of the frog, the toad. Its association is principally based on the ancient belief that it is responsible for one of the world's most common skin complaints: the wart. This old belief grew out of the coincidence that the surface of the wart resembles the toad's rough, somewhat horned skin. Further, our ancestors knew that when a toad is grabbed in the mouth of another animal—say, a dog—it gives off a fluid that irritates the predator's tissues and causes it to drop the toad. They suspected that this same fluid perhaps caused warts to grow on the hands of anyone who touched the animal.

Ever since some forgotten time children have been warned to touch neither toads nor frogs lest warts result. The cures for warts are legion, with many still in use today. Remember that in Louisiana a bag filled with alligator teeth will prevent them. A traditional European and American remedy calls for you to rub the wart with a grain of barley and then feed the grain to a chicken; somehow, the disappearance of the grain down the animal's throat marks the beginning of the wart's departure. A similar cure is found in Kentucky; this time you're to rub the wart until it bleeds, after which a drop of the blood is placed on a grain of corn and fed to a rooster. Also in Kentucky, and in New York State as well, a burial ritual is advised. Kentuckians are to rub the wart with a chicken gizzard, while New Yorkers are to twirl a strip of bacon around their heads, after which the gizzard and the bacon are to be buried; when each decays, the wart will disappear.

If the above strike you as strange, consider this one, which is found in various U.S. regions: take a dead cat to a cemetery and, holding it by the tail, swing it around your head three times in the moonlight. Your warts will disappear, never to return again.

As strange and as unscientific as these remedies are, they do have the habit of working at times, especially when the patient is young and has a deep faith in them— this because the wart is widely thought to be psychological in origin and may respond to psychological treatment.

A Final Note

For anyone who may now be smiling smugly and thinking that all the remedies we've mentioned are the province of superstitious and unsophisticated rural folk, we close with an item that continues to persist in the city as well as the countryside—the belief that the eating of fish improves the workings of the brain. Until early in our century many physicians prescribed the eating of fish for this purpose because of its phosphorus content. Science has dismissed the theory, and the whole notion has been traced back to the Christian Europe of the Middle Ages. It began when someone noticed that fish was the chief dietary staple of monks and concluded that it must be responsible for their learning and intelligence. The truth of the matter was that the monks were drawn principally from the educated classes.

COLLECTIBLES

The Small Ones

The fly that plays too long in the candle singes his wings at last.

Happy as a clam at high tide: Since clamming is done at low tide, clams are said to be the safest—and therefore the happiest—at high tide. The saying, which is especially popular in New England, is often heard simply as *happy as a clam.*

Gossips are like frogs: they drink and talk.

If a rat or mouse comes into your house, you can be rid of it by writing it a polite note requesting that it leave. Then place the note in the entrance to the little animal's hiding place.

How doth the busy little bee
Improve each shining hour,
And gather honey all the day
From every opening flower.
        —Isaac Watts (1674–1748), "Against Idleness"

If you kill one flea in March, you kill a hundred.

When you kill one fly, ten will come to its funeral.

Should you hear a cricket chirping in your house, take care not to disturb it. It will bring good luck, money, and prosperity.
        —American Ozarks

The wanton boy who kills a fly
Shall feel the spider's enmity.
                    —William Blake (1757–1827),
                            "Auguries of Innocence"

Three enemies of the body: wind, smoke, and fleas.
                            —Ireland

Ladybug, ladybug, fly away home,
Your house is on fire and your children are gone;
All but one and her name is Ann,
And she crept under the frying pan.

The ant had wings to her hurt: a caution against questing after a position beyond your means to handle.

Go to the ant, thou sluggard; consider her ways, and be wise.
                            —Proverbs

A dead mouse feels no cold.

And a variation: *A dead bee yields no honey.*

Consider the little mouse, how sagacious an animal it is which never entrusts its life to one hole only.
                    —Plautus (254–184 B.C.), *Truculentus*

Make a beeline for . . . : To head straight for someone or something.

The centipede was happy quite until a toad in fun
Said, "Pray, which leg goes after which?"
That worked her mind to such a pitch,
She lay distracted in a ditch,
Considering how to run.
                            —Mrs. Howard Craster

CHAPTER SEVEN

Of Gods and Sacred Ones

THE ANCIENTS depicted their gods in three forms—as humans, as animals, and as amalgamations of the two. As was said in the introduction to this book, literally hundreds of animals of all sizes and species and from every environ—the land, sea, and air—served as deities in antiquity. They were elevated to their exalted positions for a variety of reasons that were mentioned from time to time in subsequent chapters.

To refresh the memory, there was the deep admiration that some generated in the human heart. The Mesopotamians deified the eagle because it could do what they could not do—fly above and beyond the mountains that rose about them. Still other societies worshiped the fish because it, too, could do what no human could do—survive and flourish beneath the waters—and because ancient man seemed to suspect, as do many of us today, that the world's land creatures originally made their way up from the ocean's depths or out of its tide pools. In India the great Hindu creator god, Brahma, was often depicted as a fish.

The admiration did not restrict itself to large animals. In Egypt, for three unusual reasons, the small and ignominious, dung-eating scarab beetle was the object of widespread veneration. First, there was the similarity between the Egyptian word for the beetle—*kheprer*—and the word for Ra, their sun god and creator of all things—*khepri*. Next, there was the beetle's habit of rolling his meal of dung into a small pellet and pushing it into a previously dug hole, after which he disappeared into the hole and remained there for twenty-eight days, the length of time it took him to devour the pellet; the Egyptians noted that as he made his way toward his lair he pushed the pellet from east to west, the same course taken daily by the sun. Finally, the Egyptians had the mistaken idea that the scarab reproduced without the aid of the female, that he, as the sun did daily, rose, so to speak, of his own accord. In the Egyptian mind these reasons left no doubt that the little creature was intimately entwined with Ra and was deserving of worship. Ra himself was often depicted in the form of the scarab beetle.

Some animals, such as the crocodile and the venomous snake, were chosen because of the fear they engendered. Then, wherever ancient man looked about him, from his cave, his tent, his village, he saw some animals in great numbers. He could not help but be awed by their widespread presence, and it was but a step from that awe to adoration. The Algonquins and other Indian tribes of North America worshiped the "great hare," with their mythology claiming that he had created the world.

It was the fate of many animal gods, however, not to remain as animals throughout the entire course of their divine careers. Over the march of the centuries, their worshipers, because of the urge to better understand and identify with them, endowed them with an increasing number of human characteristics and finally transformed them completely into humans. Such was the case with one of the mightiest of all the ancient deities.

FROM EAGLE TO MAN

He began his career as an eagle. He was named the god of the sky and weather because of his ability to fly beyond the reach of the human eye and enter the heavenly realm where the drama of the elements was staged. But he has come down to us not as eagle but as the handsome, long-haired, and full-bearded man into which his

Greek worshipers eventually fashioned him. He was Zeus, the supreme god of all the deities on Mt. Olympus.

On being metamorphosed into a human, Zeus did not abandon his association with animals. The eagle he had once been remained sacred to him. Greek legend tells of how he often disguised himself as one animal or another when making his trips down to earth from Olympus for his frequent and cherished trysts with mortal women. He assumed the disguises to keep his identity from his romantic partners and to avoid the wrath of his jealous wife, Hera. For one rendezvous he arrived in the form of a swan. To Europa, the daughter of the king of Ethiopia, he appeared as a beautiful white bull as she was gathering seaside flowers. His beauty and gentleness so touched Europa that she caressed him and then, mounting his back, allowed herself to be borne off to Crete, where Zeus revealed his true self and bedded the young woman. Out of their union came three sons, one of whom, Minos, the king of Crete, we will meet in the next chapter.

The tales of Zeus' erotic adventures make entertaining reading; indeed, to the Greeks he was not only a mighty deity but also a full-blooded figure of great comedy—an early-day good ole boy—in his desperate efforts to hide his shenanigans from the jealous Hera. But the stories advance from the entertaining to the fascinating when we learn the practical reason behind their invention and telling. In common with many other ancient cultures, Egypt among them, Greece was originally the home of a collection of individual communities, each of which worshiped its own deities. It is widely thought that when the belief in Zeus spread throughout Greece, the legends had him assume his disguises as a way of gracefully taking over from the local gods by first fusing with them.

PART ANIMAL, PART HUMAN

In some societies the transformation of the animal deity to a human was never fully realized. What resulted was a worldwide collection of strange-looking gods that were part animal and part human. They are fascinating to see in the painted and carved representations that have come down to us through the ages. Ea, the Babylonian god of the waters, is represented as half man and half fish. In India Ganesha, the god of wisdom and good fortune, has the body of a man but the head of an elephant. One of the oddest of the lot is the crocodile god of Panama's Chiriqui Indians. He is variously depicted as having the legs and body of a human and the head of crocodile, or—and here he could keep you awake at night—the body of a human with a crocodile head attached to each end.

Egypt played second fiddle to no other culture when it came to deities in which the animal and the human were blended. The story of the Egyptian gods dates back some four thousand years before Christ, to a time when the nation's people were divided into tribes. Each tribe worshiped its own deity, one often in the form of an animal or a bird well known to the group. On moving out to hunt or advancing into battle, the tribal leader carried a staff atop which was perched a representation of the local god—perhaps a falcon, ram, ibis, scorpion, or jackal. Over the centuries, these gods were given human characteristics and the body of a human male or female, but were usually left with some vestige of the animals they had once been—their wings, their heads, or some part of their heads, such as the horns or ears. Though the list of the Egyptian major and minor gods is long, just five examples can give a firm idea of the varied human-animal combinations into which they were ultimately molded:

Ra, the god of the sun. He was depicted as either a hawk or a man with a hawk's head surmounted by a snake (as a symbol of supreme power) or a red disk representing the sun.

Keb, the god of the earth. Known to his worshipers as the "Great Cackler" because he was said to have helped produce the cosmic egg, the vessel of the universe, he was represented as having the head of a goose.

Horus, the god of light and the life-giving power of the sun. Like Zeus, he began life as a bird—a falcon—that, like the eagle, could fly beyond the reach of the human eye. He eventually became a falcon-headed god. Many Egyptians believed the sky to be a godly falcon whose eyes were the sun and moon.

Sekhmet, the goddess of war and vengeance. Hers was the head of a lioness.

Selket, one of the four goddesses who protected the dead. Her face and body were those of a human, but sweeping out from her arms were great wings that could be spread protectively about the tombs of the nobility.

Isis, the Egyptian goddess of the earth and moon, also did duty as a protectress of the dead. She, too, had the body and head of a human, with wings attached to her arms. According to one legend, when her godly husband, Osiris, was killed by his evil brother, Set, and his body hacked into fourteen pieces, Isis helped to put the pieces back together and breathed life into him with the gentle movement of her wings.

THE SACRED ONES

As more and more of the animal gods became human in form, the creatures they had once been were neither forgotten nor cast aside. The respect and awe in which the ancient mind held them would not allow that to happen. Instead, they became sacred to the new deities and were placed under their protection, with the eagle and Zeus being a prime case in point. In their new capacity they joined the many animals that, while never having achieved godly status themselves, were likewise revered by the people for their traits and abilities and designated as sacred to and protected by the gods.

The list of animals sacred to the ancient gods is long. Here, drawn from several cultures, are a few examples, with each followed by the name of the god by whom it was held sacred:

The bull: the Indian god Siva. Siva's bull was snow white and called Nandi. In common with many of the deities of India, Siva was seen as having a dual nature. On the one hand, he was the god of the arts, knowledge, gaiety, and dancing. On the other, he was known as the destroyer god.

The cow: Isis. In addition to being the goddess of the earth and moon, Isis symbolized the devoted wife and mother. The cow was sacred to her in great part because of the milk that the animal produced.

The dove: Venus, the Roman goddess of beauty and sensual love. Also sacred to her were the swan and the swallow.

The fox: Inari, the Japanese god (or goddess) of rice. In general, the Japanese regarded foxes as sly and malicious, but made an exception in Inari's case. His (or her) sacred animals were known as "good foxes."

The hawk: Ra, the Egyptian god of the sun. Ra was variously depicted as a hawk or a combination of the human body and the hawk's head. He was, of course, also depicted in the form of that other animal sacred to him, the lowly scarab.

The horse: Poseidon, the Greek god of the sea. He was also the god of horses and was said to maintain a stable of horses with golden manes and bronze hooves at his undersea castle. Whenever he traveled, they drew his chariot. The horse was also sacred to Mercury, the Roman messenger of the gods.

The association of the horse with Poseidon is to be found in one of the great myths concerning the god. It seems that Poseidon and Athena, the goddess of wisdom, became involved in a prolonged argument over which of the two would have the honor of naming the capital city of Attica. Their fellow gods, growing impatient with the debate, decided on a contest to settle the matter. The two would each produce a gift of value to the people, with the city then to be named for the one whose gift was judged to be more useful. Poseidon took up his trident and struck the ground with it, causing a horse to spring forth. Athena replied by creating the olive tree. The gods declared the olive tree to be the more valuable and named the city for her: Athens.

(Far to the north of Greece the horse was sacred to Frey, the Norse god of fruitfulness and the dispenser of rain and sunshine. It was said that his giant mount, Bloodyhoof, could make the ground tremble as it galloped across the earth. And as you'll recall from an earlier chapter, the magnificent, eight-legged steed, Sleipnir, was ridden by Odin, the Norse god of the wind.)

The panther: Bacchus, the Roman god of wine. Also sacred to Bacchus was that mythical monster, the dragon.

The peacock: Juno, the Roman goddess of the heavens and the protectress of women. She was the Roman counterpart of Greece's Hera, the wife of Zeus. The peacock was sacred to her because of its beauty. Also sacred to her were the goose, because of its fertility, and the raven because of its ability to fly high.

The owl: Athena of Greece and her Roman counterpart Minerva. Because the bird was found in such great number at Athens, the owl was bestowed on Athena as her symbol when the city was named in her honor. The bird then was taken by the Romans and made sacred to Minerva when they developed her out of the concept of Athena.

The stag: Diana, the Roman counterpart of Greece's Artemis, the goddess of hunting and chastity.

Many animals, while not necessarily sacred to a particular deity, were nevertheless considered sacred or supernatural by a society because they acted as servants of the gods. The great Hindu god Brahma rode a swan or goose across the sky. Numerous gods of the sky had their chariots propelled across the heavens by horses; among them was Brahma's fellow Hindu deity Indra, the god of the firmament; his chariot was pulled by thousands of horses. Greece's giant three-headed dog, Cerberus, served as a watchdog at the gates of hell for the lord of the underworld, Hades. The peoples of West Africa believed that the ant was the messenger of their serpent god. In the Nyasaland region in the continent's southeast, the chameleon and lizard were considered the messengers of God.

There, legend has it that God once sent the two animals to earth with good-news-bad-news messages concerning death. The chameleon was to carry the happy word that after death, the people would be born again, while the lizard was to inform them that there would be only nothingness after death. The lizard was the first to arrive with his grim tidings. When the chameleon arrived a short while later, the people lost their temper with him for causing them such upset by his tardiness. Their anger has never abated. It is still the native custom in Nyasaland to be angry with the chameleon and to kill the animal with tobacco juice. The lizard, thanks to his terrible message, got off no better and remains hated to this day, so much so that he scoots away in fear on glimpsing a human.

One of the most famous of the ancient messenger animals was the raven. It served in that capacity for both Odin of the Norse people and Apollo of Greece. Norse myth tells of how Odin's ravens, Munin and Hunin, would fly out from his palace each day and then return to perch on his shoulder and whisper of all that they had seen. Odin was a dual-personality deity who served, at one extreme, as the god of war and, at the other, as the god of wisdom, magic, prophecy, and poetry.

Apollo was the god of music and poetry and, in Greek mythology, is said to have given the raven its black color. It seems that Apollo loved Coronis, the mother of the god of medicine, Aesculapius, but that she was unfaithful to him with a mortal man. Apollo's messenger bird, a beautiful white raven, brought the news of her infidelity, driving the god into such a jealous rage that he had Coronis killed and then stripped the feathers from the raven, banished it to Hades, and declared that it should be colored black for all time to come.

A New Direction

The tradition of declaring animals as sacred to the gods or as sacred in themselves was one that was found in virtually all ancient societies. And it was one that did not end with antiquity. It persisted through the centuries, but, especially when the concept of a single universal deity became widespread, it took a new direction. The trend was now not to see the animals as sacred but to honor them by associating them with major religious figures. The list of such honored animals became exceedingly long in the Christian era when they were identified with Jesus Christ and the saints.

Several animals are closely associated with Christ, among them the dove, the ass, and the robin—the dove because of its appearance at the Savior's baptism (as reported in Matthew), the ass because it was the animal ridden by Jesus on the journey to Jerusalem, and the robin because of a legend of how the bird came by its red breast. (It is said that, while Christ was on the road to Calvary, a robin flew low and plucked a thorn from his terrible crown; in so doing, the bird injured itself and splashed its breast with blood.) Likewise, the stork, which is held sacred in Sweden due to the legend that it flew sorrowfully about the cross.

As for the saints, the list of animals associated with them is extremely long. Here, to show the range of animals involved, are just twelve from their ranks:

The bear:	Columba, Edmund, and Gallus.
The boar:	Emilion.
The camel:	Hormidas and Julian of Cilicia.
The crow:	Vincent.
The crocodile:	Helenus and Theodore.
The deer:	Henry.
The goose:	Martin.
The horse:	Irene and Barochus
The leopard:	Marciana.
The pig:	Anthony the Great.
The rat:	Gertrude of Nivelles.
The raven:	Benedict, Erasmus, and Paul the Hermit.

The association of certain animals with the saints came about in any of several ways. In some instances, it was based on the occupation or group that took the saint as its patron; it is because St. Anthony the Great is the patron saint of swineherds that he is always pictured with a small pig in his arms. In other instances the animal symbolized particular qualities in the religious figure or certain aspects of his or her work. Prime examples here are the animal associations made with St. Francis of Assisi, St. Luke, and St. Patrick. The association of the bird with St. Francis is based on the saint's gentleness and his habit of preaching to birds, while the ox is associated with St. Luke because his gospel begins with the priest sacrificing the animal in the Temple. St. Patrick has been traditionally mentioned in connection with snakes since the time when, so legend holds, he drove them out of Ireland.

In still other cases the association hangs on some incident in the religious figure's life; the cock, for instance, is linked with St. Peter because of its crowing at the time of Peter's denial of Christ. And then there are those cases in which legend accounts for the associations, as can be seen in the following trio of stories.

The Bee and St. Anthony of Padua

The bee is associated with St. Anthony of Padua (ca. 340–397), at one time the bishop of Milan, because of a legend surrounding the saint's infancy. According to the tale, a swarm of bees alighted on his mouth as he was lying in his crib. The odd occurrence was considered a fine omen for his future life. Anthony's emblem is the beehive.

The Eagle and St. Medard

The eagle was sacred to Jupiter, the supreme god of the Romans (also called Jove and known as the Roman counterpart of Greece's Zeus) and is associated with several saints, among them Augustine, John the Evangelist, and Medard. The legend that is told about St. Medard, a sixth-century French bishop, has it that he was standing with a group of people one day when a sudden shower sent them running for cover. Everyone but the saint was drenched. He was protected by an eagle that spread its wings over him.

The Lion and St. Jerome

Sacred to Vulcan, the Roman god of fire, the lion is associated with Saints Mark, Adrian, and Jerome. The connection with Jerome (ca. 340–420) stems from the tale of how a lion once entered a classroom in which the saint was lecturing. All the students fled, but Jerome remained. On seeing that the lion was limping, he took up the animal's paw and found a thorn embedded in it. Gently, the saint removed the thorn, bathed the wound, and wrapped it with a bandage. In gratitude the lion asked to become his faithful companion. The saint is usually depicted as an old man dressed as a cardinal and sitting deep in study with a lion alongside him.

It is fitting to end this chapter with three stories from centuries gone by. They open the way to a chapter composed almost entirely of stories that date from deep in antiquity to the present and that fully deserve the title the chapter has given them—Fabulous Tales All.

COLLECTIBLES

Potpourri

Three things not to be trusted: a cow's horn, a dog's tooth, and a horse's hoof.
—Ireland and England

He that has a white horse and a fair wife never wants trouble.

Because a Donkey takes a whim
To Bray at you, why Bray at him?
—Arthur Guiterman, *A Poet's Proverbs*

Would you like to make cod liver oil taste better? Then drink a glass of water in which you've placed some nails and given them time to rust. The cod liver oil will take on the taste of fresh oysters.
—American south

The above is just fine if you happen to like oysters. Otherwise you'd best be content with what you've got.

It is the worthless hen that fails to provide for herself.

The bluebird carries the sky on his back.
—Henry David Thoreau (1817–1862), *Journal*

As faithful as the chameleon's skin: A satiric reference to untrustworthiness, based on the chameleon's ability to change its colors.

145

Who killed Cock Robin?
"I," said the Sparrow,
"With my bow and arrow,
I killed Cock Robin."

> —Anonymous,
> "The Death and Burial of Cock Robin"

Cats and monkeys, monkeys and cats—all human life is there.

> —Henry James (1843–1916),
> "The Madonna of the Future"

A wren in the hand is better than a crane to be caught: An Irish variation of *a bird in the hand is worth two in the bush.*

With Latin, a horse, and money, a man may travel the world.

Whistling girls and crowing hens
Always come to some bad ends.

> —New England

If you wish to make a crow talk, you can do so by splitting its tongue.

Swans hatch their eggs only during storms. Thunder and lightning break open the shells.

> —old British superstition

If you rub a cat the wrong way and see sparks, cold weather is in the making.

> —New England

Between dog and wolf: An aged and almost forgotten phrase referring to dusk.

It is a sorry flock where the ewe bears the bell: Another old and almost forgotten saying, this one from England. It holds that the home run solely by the wife is an unfortunate one.

Wild elephants are caught by tame;
With money it is just the same.
                    —Pilpay, *The Panchatantra*

If you ride a horse, sit close and tight,
If you ride a man, sit easy and light.
                    —Benjamin Franklin

CHAPTER EIGHT

Fabulous Tales All

THOUGH THE HUMAN IMAGINATION is everywhere present in animal folklore, nowhere does it climb to greater heights or extend over a broader field than in the tales. They are tales—myths, legends, and fables—in which the themes range from the mightiest to the most commonplace and in which the animals play various and, at times, sharply contrasting roles. In some, the animals are assigned major parts in grand theories of how the world was created. In others, however, they are not magnificent creative beings but rather strange and sometimes terrifying creatures that are vanquished by the great heroes of legend. And, finally, they perform as central characters in the myriad fables that, beginning with those of Aesop, contain insights and simple morals whose timelessness make them able to guide us today in our everyday affairs.

AT THE CREATION

In attempting to explain creation, the ancients did not limit themselves to tales of the beginnings of the world itself. The tales also sought to explain the creation of humans, animals, and the foodstuffs needed to sustain life.

The animal tales of creation usually shared two points in common. First, they were based on the belief that the sea was present long before the land took shape, indicating, as was said earlier, that the ancients seemed to suspect that the world's land creatures originally made their way up from ocean's depths or out of its tide pools. Second, the animals were chosen for the tales for the very same reasons that certain animals were worshiped as gods; they were the creatures that were admired or feared by the people of a culture.

These two points—one or the other, or both—are present in the following legends of how the peoples of widely separated regions, in the absence of even the most rudimentary of scientific knowledge and paraphernalia, accounted for the creation of their world, themselves, and the riches in the nature around them.

The World: Jumala Ukko

The greatest of all the gods, Jumala Ukko, sent an eagle or a wild duck (both deeply admired because of their ability to do what no man could do: fly) to his daughter, Ilmater, the goddess of air. Nestling in the lap of the goddess, who had been floating in space for seven hundred years, the bird laid seven eggs. Ilmater then traveled to the depths of the ocean and, from the eggs, created heaven and then the earth, with its continents, islands, mountains, and valleys. The tale comes to us from Finland.

The World: Lakhmu and Lakhmanu

A legend from the mythology of the Assyrian and Babylonian cultures that flourished in the region between the Tigris and Euphrates rivers tells us that at first, there were only the waters—Apsu, the primordial ocean, and Tiamat, the tempestuous sea. In time, these waters came together. Their mingling produced two giant serpents, Lakhmu and Lakhamu, who gave birth to Anshar and Kishar. The two offspring were, respectively, the celestial sky and the terrestial earth. From them came all the great gods of the world and underworld.

The World: Of Birds and Turtles

In India legend has it that an amphibious creature—often said to be a bird—dove deep into the sea and fetched up a bit of mud that eventually became the earth. The Mandan Indians, a now-extinct tribe that once lived along North America's upper Missouri River, believed that two pigeons flew back and forth across the waters until a blade of grass appeared below them, after which the land emerged.

While viewed as a creator by a number of ancient societies, the turtle, because of the strength of his shell, was more often depicted as the animal who supported the world on his back. As such, he figures prominently in a creation tale told by several North American Indian tribes, among them the Delaware and Iroquois. To understand the story it is necessary to know that the tribes believed that a world similar to ours had existed for all time somewhere in the sky. A young woman named Ataentsic became the bride of the chief god there and bore him a child, only to find that he was insanely jealous of her and a fellow god, having come to suspect that the infant was the product of their mating. In his fury he cast Ataentsic and the child out of his world and sent them plunging down through the sky.

As Ataentsic fell she sighted a lake far below, a lake so vast that it was without boundaries. Living in its waters were the turtle, the otter, and the muskrat. On sighting the approaching figures, the animals decided to dive to the bottom of the lake and dredge up some earth so that it would provide the newcomers with a landing place. Only the muskrat succeeded in doing so, returning to the surface and placing a mouthful of mud on the turtle's shell. Instantly the shell began to grow and became our world. When Ataentsic and her child neared the new land, they were caught by birds and safely deposited there. Ataentsic became the dawn and later created the sun and moon.

Humans: The Serpent God's Journey

The plumed-serpent god traveled to the underworld, or Mictlan as it was called. There, he came upon the bones of people who had lived in worlds that had existed before the present one took shape. He carried the bones back to the surface and sprinkled them with his own blood. They turned into human beings. The god was Quetzalcoatl, the great deity of the Aztec Indians of Mexico.

Humans: The Egg

The myths of one nation tell of how its social classes were hatched from eggs of different metals. Emerging from eggs of gold were the country's chieftains; from silver eggs, the nobility; and from copper eggs, the common people. The nation: Peru.

Humans: The Mockingbird

All the world's people made their way to the earth's surface from the subterranean lake called Sipapu. On emerging into the open, they were greeted by a mockingbird. Singing all the while, the bird assigned each individual a tribe and a language. When the songs ended, the unfortunates who had not yet been given a tribe and a language descended back into a nether gloom. The story is told by the Hopi Indians of the southwestern United States.

Foods: The Eel

The people of the Pacific's Tonga delight in this tale of how one of their principal food sources came into existence:

A male eel—called Eel—was born of a human couple and, after a time spent living in a pool, swam to Samoa, where he again took up life in a pool. One day a young maiden, a virgin, became pregnant because she swam too near Eel, an incident that caused the Samoans to decide to kill him. On the eve of his execution, however,

Eel told the girl to have the people cut off his head after his death and bury it. His instructions were heeded and soon the first coconut tree sprang forth from the head's burial place.

The story says much about the commonality of the human mind. The eel served many ancient island people in much the same capacity as the serpent served the continental people. Both animals functioned as fertility and creative symbols, in great part because of their phallic shapes. Though the two peoples had (as far as we know) no contact, each hit upon the same characteristics.

Animals: Ahura Mazda's Ox

Persian myth tells this story of how the animals themselves were first born.

The god of wisdom, Ahura Mazda, created a huge ox, an animal that greatly disturbed him when it turned out to be a raging, senseless monster incapable of giving the world anything of value. A fellow deity, the young and handsome Mithra, came upon the ox, grabbed it by the horns, flung himself upon its back, and broke the beast's will. Though initially planning to do it no harm, Mithra was ordered by the sun to kill the animal. He obediently drew his knife from its sheath. A moment later the ox toppled in a heap, with blood spurting from its neck. From that blood and the dying creature's limbs emerged all the world's animal species.

Animals: Sedna's Fingers

Here, from the Eskimos, is the grim tale of how the creatures of the sea originated.

There was once a beautiful Eskimo maiden named Sedna, who fell in love with a handsome stranger and eloped with him in his canoe. Her father, disconsolate over her sudden and unannounced departure and fearful that he would never see her again, set out to find her. When he at last came upon his daughter on a distant island, he learned that she now loathed her lover because he had revealed himself to be not a human but a bird spirit. She willingly stole away with her father and began the long journey home.

But the bird spirit pursued the fleeing pair. Overtaking their boat, he created a violent storm that terrified the father—so terrified the old man, indeed, that he thrust Sedna overboard as a sacrifice to appease the spirit and thus end the storm. Fighting for her life, Sedna clutched the side of the boat, only to have her father take up his ax and chop off her fingers. The girl disappeared beneath the boiling waves, but struggled back to the surface three times and again clutched at the boat. On each occasion the ax came crashing down to mutilate her hands. She finally vanished from sight for good.

Out of this terrible incident were born the creatures of the sea. Sedna's severed fingers became fish, and her crushed knuckles became deep-sea seals, walruses, and whales.

Animals: Of Alligators and Buzzards

There are even tales of how various animals came to have their distinguishing physical characteristics. Here are two related by North America's Indians.

The Creek tell the story of what happened when the alligator god was playing ball with some birds and the eagle and turkey gods. The alligator held the ball in his jaws and would not release it, causing the eagle to pounce on his nose and break it. The alligator's jaws opened wide in pain, whereupon the turkey grabbed the ball away and enabled the birds to win the game. The break eventually healed but left a dent in its stead. To this day all alligators have that distinctive dent in their snouts.

From the Hopi comes the legend of why the buzzard is bald. It all happened at the beginning of time, when the sun was being raised into the sky. The blazing orb became stuck long before it reached its proper height. With its heat too great for the survival of the people, desperate attempts were made to push it still higher. When they ended in failure, the buzzard flew aloft. Immediately all the feathers on his head were burned away, but he refused to retreat and, fighting off the awful pain, eased the sun higher and higher until it was at last where it belonged. His descendants have never been able to grow feathers on their heads.

THE VANQUISHED ONES

At this point we must turn from those animal figures honored as creators to those whose destiny it was to be brought to their knees by the heroic figures in the legends of old.

Virtually every antique culture, from the most primitive to the most advanced, boasted its legendary heroes, those strong men who performed magnificent—and quite impossible—feats of daring and courage. Improbable though the adventures of these superhuman figures may have been, they served the ancient in several very practical ways. They gave him a pride in his culture; they encouraged him to be himself brave in a too-often hostile environment; they taught him that evil, lurking within himself or in the surrounding world, must be faced and overcome; and they taught him that, to survive, he must conquer the elements.

The exploits of so many of the legendary heroes involved face to face encounters with monsters or fearsome animals. The Greek hero Perseus saved the life of the beautiful Andromeda, the daughter of the king of Ethiopia, and won her hand in marriage by slaying a dragon (a feat that was reflected in the later Western European legend of St. George's victory over a dragon). To the north and west the Celtic hero Cu Chulainn started on the way to becoming the guardian of the kingdom of Ulster when, as a child of seven years, he killed a fierce watchdog. Several North American Indian tribes and the people of Scandinavia and Iceland all shared the myth that the world's violent winds, which were believed to be caused by the endless flapping of a giant bird's wings, were brought under control by a hero figure. Here, as told by the Micmac Indians of southeastern Canada, is one version of that myth.

Gluskabe and the Great Bird

The people who lived alongside the great waters were starving because heavy winds and storms kept them from going out to fish. They were reduced to wandering along the beaches in search of any fish that might have been cast up by the angry waves. Among the wanderers was the great hero of their culture, Gluskabe. One day, after wandering far along the beach, he came upon a rocky outcropping just offshore upon which a massive bird sat beating its wings. Realizing that here was the cause of the unending winds, Gluskabe approached the bird and tricked the animal into thinking it was shivering with cold, after which Gluskabe carried the creature across a series of rocks to the shore, ostensibly to find a place of warmth for it.

As he struggled beneath his burden Gluskabe carefully stepped from boulder to boulder. But when one last rock separated him from the beach, he pretended to stumble. Down he went as he had planned all along, causing the bird to break one of its wings. Gluskabe then shepherded the injured animal the rest of the way to safety, bandaged its wing, and warned it that it must not flap the limb again until the break was healed.

The winds died and Gluskabe's people were able to begin fishing again. But soon they were in even greater trouble than before, this time because there was no wind whatsoever. The heat became unbearable, and the waters so oily and clouded over that the fishermen could not glimpse their prey beneath the surface. So back to the wounded bird Gluskabe's people went. They undid the bandages and set the creature free. But to avoid reinjuring itself and to help the people, they urged the bird not to flap its wings violently ever again. The grateful animal did as requested, and for the most part the winds have been controlled and good and gentle to the people ever since.

The Labors of Heracles

Possibly the greatest of all the legendary heroes was Heracles of Greece, a figure better known to us by his Roman name, Hercules. Conceived out of wedlock to Zeus and the mortal Alcmene during one of the god's many earthly trysts, he showed his great strength and courage early—in fact, he displayed them right at birth. Hera, the goddess wife of Zeus, hating the children that her husband's notorious dalliances with mortals produced, sent two serpents to destroy the infant when he was just a few minutes old. The attempt ended in death for the serpents when Heracles' tiny but awesomely strong hands strangled them both in his crib.

As spectacular as it was, the feat was as nothing when compared with the great works that Heracles was assigned in his young manhood. Numbering twelve in all, they were imposed as punishments after he had killed his three children in a fit of madness inflicted on him by the still-wrathful Hera. Of the twelve labors ten involved animals.

The First Labor: The Nemean Lion

The labors were ordered by the young man's cousin Eurystheus, the king of Mycenae. The first pitted Heracles against a savage lion that, roaming the distant valley of Nemea, was the offspring of the hundred-headed monster, Typhon. On being instructed to bring Eurystheus the lion's skin, Heracles made his way to the valley, only to find that his arrows and club did the beast not one whit of harm. The young man then cast the weapons aside, attacked the lion with his bare hands, and strangled him to death.

The Second Labor: The Lernean Hydra

This task sent Heracles against another child of Typhon—a poisonous nine-headed water snake that was ravaging the countryside of Lernea. At first the young man seemed doomed to failure. He attacked the creature's heads, but every time he hacked one off, it immediately sprouted two in its place. To get the job done Heracles had to enlist the help of his nephew Iolaus. Now, each time he severed one of the heads, he sent Iolaus dashing forward with a flaming torch to burn the stump and create a seal that kept the new heads from growing. Defeat came at last to the monstrous snake when its middle head, which was said to be immortal, was severed. Heracles buried the head beneath a giant boulder to keep it from ever escaping.

The Third Labor: The Arcadian Stag

For his third task Heracles was told not to kill an animal but to bring it back alive to Eurystheus. The target was the beautiful Arcadian stag, an animal with golden antlers and bronze feet. The stag was sacred to Artemis (better known to us by her Roman name, Diana), the goddess of hunting and chastity. The fleet animal avoided Heracles for more than a year before being wounded by one of his arrows. Once the stag was captured, Heracles trekked home with his prey flung across his shoulder.

The Fourth Labor: The Erymanthian Boar

Again, Heracles was ordered to bring a dreaded animal back alive—this time an ugly and fierce boar that lived on the slopes of Mt. Erymanthia. The hunter accomplished his task by throwing a net over the animal after an exhausting chase through the snow. On being taken to Mycenae, the beast so terrified Eurystheus that the king ordered Heracles to keep all his future captives outside the gates of the city.

The Fifth Labor: The Augean Stables

Of all the Heraclean labors, the assignment to clean the stables of Augeas, the king of the Epean people, is the only one that has a comic ring to it. To be cleaned in a single day were stable yards and stalls that were home to the king's three thousand oxen and that had not been cleaned in thirty years. Heracles accomplished his task in a clever way. Rather then picking up a shovel, he diverted the waters of the nearby Alpheus and Peneus rivers and sent them cascading through the yards and stalls.

The Sixth Labor: The Stymphalian Birds

The young man was now dispatched to Lake Stymphalis, there to kill or drive away a flock of man-eating birds that had been reared by Ares, the god of war. Always ravenously hungry, the birds were equipped with beaks, wings, and claws of brass, and with arrowlike feathers that they fired at their prey—or anyone else—at the slightest provocation. They, however, had a weak side to their nature and could be frightened by an enemy. Heracles took advantage of their weakness and put them to flight by shaking a brass rattle. Then he downed them with well-aimed arrows.

The Seventh Labor: The Cretan Bull

The Cretan Bull was a magnificent white creature that belonged to Minos, the king of Crete. The beast came into being when Minos asked Poseidon, the god of the sea, to fetch him a bull for sacrifice. Poseidon obliged by bringing the animal up from the ocean depths. Its beauty was such, however, that Minos decided to keep it for himself and sacrificed another animal in its place. Heracles' task was to capture the Cretan Bull and carry it to Mycenae, a job that he accomplished by besting the animal in hand-to-hand combat and then slinging him over his shoulder for the trek home. Soon after his arrival he set the bull free. It roamed the Greek countryside, wreaking havoc all the while, until it met its death at the hands of another legendary Greek hero, Theseus.

One of the most memorable aspects of the Cretan Bull's story is the action taken by Poseidon on hearing that Minos had kept the animal for himself. Enraged at what he saw as a trick against his divine person, Poseidon drove the beast wild and caused Minos' wife to fall in love with it. The two mated, with the union producing the Minotaur, a monster with the head of a bull and the body of a man. Instead of commanding that the hideous offspring be killed, Minos had the famed Labyrinth built and placed the Minotaur in it. For years thereafter seven Greek youths and seven maidens were sent there annually as sacrifices to its ravenous appetite for human flesh. The Minotaur, as did its sire, eventually met its death at the hands of the hero Theseus.

The Eighth Labor: The Wild Mares of Diomedes

These were wild, flesh-eating horses owned by Diomedes, the king of the Bistone people in Thrace. Heracles experienced little trouble in capturing the animals and, as ordered by Eurystheus, starting them on their way back to Mycenae. Trouble arrived, however, when the pursuing Diomedes and his troops overtook Heracles and attacked him. Heracles was unable to fight off the onslaught and control the horses at the same time, and so he placed them in the care of his friend and companion Abderus. The strategy proved a mistake, for the animals immediately tore their new keeper to bits and devoured him. The setback, however, was but a temporary one. Heracles killed Diomedes in battle, put his troops to flight, and then fed the king's flesh to the mares. They immediately became docile and caused him no trouble during the remainder of the journey home. Once they had been exhibited to Eurystheus, Heracles set them free. They roamed the slopes of Mt. Olympus before finally losing their lives to beasts far wilder than they.

Heracles then went about his ninth—and first

nonanimal-related—labor. In a quest that took him through Europe and Asia, he secured the girdle that gave Hippolyte, the queen of a race of warrior women called the Amazons, her great power.

The Tenth Labor: The Oxen of Geryon

Owned by Geryon, a winged monster with three heads and three bodies, these oxen were to be found on a mythical island, Erythia, far to the west of Mycenae. It was known as the "red island" because it was said to be under the rays of the setting sun. The oxen likewise were said to be red. They were guarded by the giant Eurytion and by yet another offspring of Typhon, the two-headed dog Orthrus. Heracles' orders: release the oxen and bring them to Eurytheus.

It was an assignment that saw him kill Eurytion and Orthrus, after which he was pursued and overtaken by Geryon. The two engaged in a to-the-death battle, with Heracles finally emerging the victor. Legend holds that the remainder of the hero's journey home took him through Gaul, Italy, Illyricum, and Thrace. On being handed over to Eurystheus, the cattle were slaughtered and offered in sacrifice to Hera.

Heracles' eleventh—and second nonanimal-related—labor sent him in search of the Golden Apples, which were said to give man immortality. There are several versions of how he successfully completed this task. One holds that he was unable to secure the treasured fruits before slaying Ladon, the dragon of one hundred heads who guarded them.

The Twelfth Labor: Cerberus

As is fitting for a climactic tale, the story of the young man's final labor involves the greatest danger of all. He was dispatched to the underworld, there to capture and bring home Cerberus, the three-headed dog that stood guard over the region. On reaching his destination, Heracles met Hades, the prince of darkness, and informed him of his mission. Hades nodded and said that the visitor was welcome to Cerberus—that is, if he could subdue the animal with his bare hands only. Heracles accepted the challenge, threw himself at Cerberus, evaded the beast's snapping jaws, wrestled the animal into his arms, and tied it securely with a rope. Hades acknowledged the hero's victory and allowed him to return to Mycenae with his captive. After allowing Eurytheus to see the animal, Heracles returned Cerberus to his underworld home.

THE FABLED ONES

The twelve labors of Heracles may be the most famous of the hero legends, but their fame cannot compare with that won by the fables of Aesop, the more than two hundred stories that have come down to us from some six centuries before Christ and that are known and respected worldwide for their simple, timeless, and universal moral precepts. They are famous in animal lore because the vast majority of them employ animals to make their points and to illustrate our human characteristics and failings.

Credited to Aesop are between 231 and 256 tales. We must say "credited" for two reasons. First, there exists such a paucity of information about the man that we cannot be certain whether he was an actual person, a legendary figure, or a collection of writers (whose works before or after his time were attributed to him). What little has been written about him borders on the legendary and holds that he was likely a Greek. His birthplace is given variously as the island of Samos and the regions of Thrace, Lydia, and Phrygia. He is said to have been born sometime around 620 B.C. and to have died in about 564 B.C. Legend has it that he spent part of his life as the slave to two monarchs in Samos, was freed by one out of gratitude for his services, and then became an adviser and assistant to Croesus, the fabulously rich king of Lydia.

Second, we do not know whether Aesop (or the writers "assembled" under his name) invented the fables or adapted them from folk legends. There are some strong arguments in favor of the latter possibility. Of all the fables attributed to his pen, one fourth have been traced to the lore of India, and thirteen to the *Jataka*, an assemblage of more than five hundred stories that Buddhists say are accounts by the Buddha (ca. 563–483 B.C.) of his former births. The remainder are said to be from early Greek lore.

But no matter their origin, the Aesopian fables have provided generations of readers with simple precepts for the conduct of their lives and their dealings with others. That the precepts and the animals employed to drive them home are many and varied can readily be seen in a sampling of just four tales.

The Fox and the Raven

The Raven is sitting in a tree and holding a piece of cheese in her beak. The Fox passes by and, quietly eyeing the cheese, compliments the Raven on the beauty of her wings and talons, but then expresses sorrow that such a fine bird is without voice. The Raven, complimented by such flattery, opens her mouth to caw. The cheese drops to the ground, where it is immediately gobbled up by the Fox. The moral: a flatterer is not to be trusted and embraced as a friend.

The Eagle and the Arrow

A bowman unleashed an arrow that struck the Eagle in the heart. The Eagle, as he was dying, turned his head in agony and saw that the tail of the arrow was equipped with his own feathers. The moral is contained in the Eagle's last words: "How much sharper are the wounds made by weapons which we ourselves have supplied!"

The Lion, the Mouse, and the Fox

One day, as the Lion was sleeping in his den, the Mouse awakened him by running over his mane and ears. Angry at being roused from his nap, the Lion searched every corner of his den to find the Mouse. The Fox, on seeing and misunderstanding the Lion's upset, chided him for being afraid of the Mouse, to which the Lion replied that he did not fear the Mouse but resented "his familiarity and ill-breeding." The moral: take not little liberties; they are great offenses.

The Monkeys and Their Mother

The Monkey gave birth to two children. One she loved deeply, fondling and nursing it with the greatest of care. The other she hated and neglected. The loved one was in time smothered by the mother's love, while the unloved one grew up despite the mother's neglect. The moral: the best intentions do not always ensure success.

The Aesopian fables do not limit themselves to precepts of use to the individual. Many also deal with political cautions of value to any nation, as witness the following tales.

The Horse and the Stag

The Horse was angry when the meadow, which he had always had to himself, was entered and damaged by the Stag. The Horse, wanting to take revenge on the intrusion, asked the Man if he would help him punish the Stag. The Man replied in the affirmative, but said that he would do so only if he were allowed to put a bit in the Horse's mouth and then ride him. The Horse agreed to the provision, only to become the slave of the Man for all time to come. The moral: revenge is too dear a purchase if its price is liberty.

The Ass and the Old Shepherd

As the Shepherd was watching his Ass feeding in a meadow, he was alarmed to hear the sounds of the approaching enemy. He begged the Ass to flee with him before they were captured, whereupon the animal asked if it would be made to carry two panniers when taken by the enemy. When the Shepherd replied yes, the Ass commented that as long it had to carry two panniers, ''What matters it to me which master I serve?'' The moral: when governments change, the poor change nothing but their masters.

Aesop is also the father of a number of animal sayings that have survived a span of some 2,600 years and remain in widespread use today. A prime example here is the expression *to take the lion's share*. It got its start in the story of the day that the Lion, Fox, Ass, and Wolf all went hunting together and killed a stag. When the moment came to divide the prey among the hunters, the Lion cut it into four equal shares. Then he demanded that he be given three fourths of the prize—one fourth because of his prerogative, one fourth for his superior courage, and one fourth for his dam and cubs. Having made his demand, he stared at his companions and challenged them to battle him for the remaining share. Intimidated by the Lion's size and fierce demeanor, they surrendered to his ultimatum and silently stole away.

Though Aesop is indisputably the world's best-known fabulist, he was joined over the centuries by many fellow practitioners, most of whom continued his practice of using animals to make his moral and political points. Among their number are some of the most distinguished figures in literary history—Russia's Leo Tolstoy (1828–1910), with his ''Jackals and the Elephant'' warning of the evil that can befall rulers who make impossible demands on their subjects; France's Anatole France (1844–1924), cautioning against the dangers of a blind and too zealous patriotism in ''Hurrah for the Penguins''; Great

Britain's Robert Louis Stevenson (1850-1894), wryly sniping at the snobbishness of English colonials in "The Carthorses and the Saddlehorse"; and the Anglo-Irish satirist Jonathan Swift (1667-1745), with his tale of "The Miser's Jackdaw" commenting that men are willing to be laughed at for their wit, but not for their folly.

(Incidentally, Swift, in the most famous of his works, *Gulliver's Travels*, a fantasy and political satire rather than a fable, made a few nasty observations about humans by comparing them with a breed of remarkable horses. In the latter stages of the book his hero finds himself in a strange land ruled by horses called the Houyhnhnms. They are the most intelligent and benevolent of creatures—far superior to the Yahoos, the race of semihumans who serve them. In their domain such man-made niceties as war and law courts are unknown and unnecessary. Their sensibilities are deeply shocked when Gulliver describes the practices and institutions of the people back in his native England.)

Britisher William Caxton (ca. 1422-1491), while not himself a fabulist, must be ranked among their number. It was he who gave England its first printing press and who, after years spent in the Low Countries, translated into English (from the Dutch) and published *The Historye of Reynart the Foxe*. The fox, with his name today spelled Reynard, was the wily, unscrupulous, lying, immoral, and traitorous central figure in a series of fables satirizing life and politics in medieval Europe. He was beloved by the people of Germany, France, the Netherlands, and then England because he defied, tricked, and made a mockery of the ideals and institutions of the day.

The United States has produced its fair share of fabulists. For those of us of appropriate vintage it seems just yesterday that humorist James Thurber (1894-1961) was delighting us with his seriocomic counsels in *Fables of Our Time*. Earlier, there was short-story writer Ambrose Bierce (1842-ca. 1914) remarking cynically on the laziness and slovenliness of our kind in "The Pig Transformed to a Man." And still earlier there was philosopher Ralph Waldo Emerson (1803–1882), turning fabulist for a moment and commenting on the value of individual differences in his verse simply titled "Fable":

> The mountain and the squirrel
> Had a quarrel,
> And the former called the latter "Little Prig";
> Bun replied,
> "You are doubtless very big;
> But all sorts of things and weather
> Must be taken in together,
> To make up a year
> And a sphere.
> And I think it no disgrace
> To occupy my place.
> If I'm not as large as you,
> You are not as small as I,
> And not half so spry.
> I'll not deny you make
> A very pretty squirrel track;
> Talents differ; all is well and wisely put;
> If I cannot make forests on my back,
> Neither can you crack a nut."

Joel Chandler Harris (1848–1908) must not be overlooked. Though he is usually not thought of as a fabulist but as one of America's finest folklorists, his use of Brer Rabbit in many of his stories qualifies him, at least in the opinion of this one writer, as a fabulist. For centuries before Harris put him to paper Brer Rabbit played a role in folklore. He can be found in tales told in Tibet, India, Burma, and Africa of how the wily little animal tricked and outwitted a variety of larger adversaries, including the elephant, lion, snake, and tiger. It was the rabbit's role in life to represent the oppressed peoples of the world—among them the black American slave—and to bolster their spirits and instill in them a sense of their own worth. He did so by besting the oppressors with the only tools available to the underdog—cunning and trickery. It was in this role that the age-old character appeared in Harris's charming tales.

Together, Aesop and Harris, so widely separated in time, bring us back full circle to Chapter One and the childhood in which we first encountered animal folklore and first read or were told the stories of the two writers. Ever since those wondrous years the folklore has been a part of our lives. It will go on being a part of our lives for the rest of our days, just as it will be a part of the lives of our children and then of their children.

WHERE THEY CAME FROM

A Glossary of Other Animal Expressions and Their Origins

THE ENGLISH LANGUAGE is sprinkled with expressions inspired by what we humans have seen of the animal world. Some are original to the language, while others have been borrowed. The origins of most have long been lost in the mists of time. But there are many whose earliest usages have been traced and pinpointed. Here now, divided between some now forgotten and some still in common use, is a selection of the more interesting of their number.

A

Alligator: A general term for a friend, either spoken to or of someone supposedly "sharp" or knowledgeable, such as in the twentieth-century expression *see you later, alligator*. In early American slang it referred to hardy, manly individuals and stemmed from the battles in which southern backwoodsmen and boatmen were said to have engaged with the beasts.

Ape: Today, an ugly and clumsy person. The term comes from the Great Britain of the Middle Ages and originally meant a fool or a dupe.

To Ape: This expression, which means "to imitate," dates back to the 1200s in Great Britain. In the 1960s the phrase *to go ape* became a popular slang to describe the act of becoming highly, even violently, emotional. *To go ape over* was concocted at about the same time to describe great enthusiasm. The vulgar *to go apeshit* was used by the military in Vietnam for emotionalism bordering on the insane.

Arachne's Labors: The term comes from the story of the fine Greek weaver Arachne who challenged the goddess of wisdom, Athena, to a weaving contest. When Arachne fashioned a web of beautiful design, Athena became so envious that she tore the work to pieces. Brokenhearted at having her effort destroyed, Arachne hanged herself, after which Athena transformed her into a spider. Thus is was that *arachnida* became the scientific name for spiders, mites, and scorpions.

The Ass Waggeth His Ears: Almost forgotten today, this saying was once meant for those who talked as if they possessed great wisdom and refined tastes but were actually without learning. The saying is linked to the old belief that the ass had no ear for music but still wagged its ears at the sound of a tune. The belief, in its turn, is connected to the ancient tale in which the Greek gods Apollo and Pan asked Midas (the legendary king who requested that the gods turn all that he touched into gold) to settle their argument over which of two made the better music on their pipes. On giving his vote to Pan, Midas so enraged Apollo that the god turned his ears into those of an ass.

B

Bantam: A species of diminutive fowl renowned for the pugnacity of its roosters, hence its application to small individuals of strong fighting spirit. Though some authorities suspect that the word may have originated in Japan, it is more widely thought to have come from Java. There, the breed of fowl was called bantam, and it was from there that it was introduced to the world. The term was applied to the soldiers of World War I who served in British units made up of men below average height. Today, it also describes a weight classification in boxing.

Bear-Leader: Virtually unheard of today, this was the eighteenth-century name given to one who conducted wealthy young men on the Grand Tour, the journey through Europe that marked their passage into manhood. The name was derived from the showmen who led muzzled bears about the streets and made them perform for coins thrown by passersby.

Bird: In modern British slang, a young woman, usually not one held in high regard. The word dates back to the 1200s, when the English used it, without any implied criticism, to mean a maiden or a young girl. It seems to have had no connection at that time with the feminine grace of flying birds, but is thought to have emerged from the Old English word for a young woman, *burde*.

Birdie: To complete a golf hole in one stroke under par (the average score listed for a hole). The term derives from the old idea that birds, because of their ability to fly, were superior creatures. Early-nineteenth-century slang substituted *bird* for very good or excellent. The slang usage went out of style later on, but remained in golf.

In golf the term *eagle* describes a hole completed in two strokes under par. Again, the idea of superiority is in evidence, but this time a greater superiority, what with the eagle having long enjoyed the reputation of being one of the most majestic of birds.

Bug: Long used to designate any insect or germ, this word may date back to the Great Britain of the fourteenth century and may have been derived from the Welsh word for ghost, *bwg*, or from the early English words *bugge* and *budde*, with the former referring variously to a demon or a scarecrow and the latter meaning beetle. It originally meant a goblin, specter, or bogey (a terrifying apparition). Out of it emerged expressions that have been with us for centuries—*bugbear* (a scarecrow in the form of a bear), *bugaboo* (an ogre or monster and, more recently, a detested task that won't go away), *bogeyman*, and *hobgoblin*.

The use of *bug* to designate insects and germs can be traced to sixteenth-century England. Since then, it has served as the root for a wide variety of expressions, among them *buggy* (crazy or infested with insects), *bughouse* (since the turn of this century, an American slang term for an insane asylum and, in England, a cheap cinema house), *firebug* (a U.S. term for a pyromaniac), *jitterbug* (a popular dance of the 1930s and 1940s, and, earlier, a crazed person), *flu bug* (an infectious germ, also sometimes called a *tummy bug*), *bug off* (a rude invitation to leave), and *to bug* (pester someone). In two of its latest uses *bug* refers to a wiretapping device or to something awry in a piece of equipment. In connection with the former we now have *to bug a room*, meaning to equip it with a listening device.

Bugger: Now referring to a worthless person, a cad, or a rascal, this word originally meant a sodomite and was first used in sixteenth-century Great Britain. It also meant a heretic and, in that context, may have come from France or Eastern Europe. Today, it is at times used affectionately, especially when referring to a rascally child.

Bull and Bull Session: Both these expressions are American slang terms of the twentieth century, though the former may stem from the seventeenth-century word *bull*, which meant jest, or the early military vulgarism *bullshit*. Whatever the case, *bull* currently means anything from nonsense to an exaggerated and often unsubstantiated point of view. *Bull session*, in use since the 1920s, means a meeting, usually of men, in which various subjects are discussed at length regardless of how expert the opinions expressed may be. Quite often, the discussions devolve into tales or claims of sexual prowess. At all times the participants are said to be *slinging the bull*.

C

To Fight Like Kilkenny Cats: Meaning to battle on until both sides have lost, this saying comes from a story told of a troop of Hessian soldiers who were garrisoned at Kilkenny, Ireland, during the rebellion of 1798. It seems that the soldiers enjoyed tying two cats together by their tails, suspending them across a clothesline, and then watching them fight. An officer, objecting to the cruel sport, ordered that it be stopped, but was disobeyed. One day, as the cats were flailing away at each other, he was sighted approaching the barracks, whereupon one soldier cut the animals away from their tails with his sword and let them escape. When the officer saw the two tails hanging from line and asked what had become of the cats, he was jokingly told that they had fought so hard that they had eaten each other.

To Grin Like a Cheshire Cat: The origin of this British simile is unknown. One old story has it that Cheshire cheese was once fashioned in the shape of cats before being sent to market, with the faces of the cats being molded so that they seemed to be smiling. But why the smiles? The story has it that the cats were amused by the idea that Cheshire was a County Palatine, the province of an earl palatine, a noble with quasi-royal powers. Six British counties were designated Counties Palatine in the wake of the Norman Conquest. Of their number only Cheshire, Durham, and Lancaster still retain the title.

Another often-mentioned possibility is that an aristocratic family in Cheshire had a lion on its crest and ordered a painter to adorn the signs on the local inns with it. The painter was perhaps none too talented or perhaps uncertain of what a lion looked like, with the result being that the signs all bore animals that resembled a grinning cat.

The simile was mentioned in the works of British satirist Peter Pindar (John Wolcot, 1738–1819) and was made world famous by Lewis Carroll (Charles Lutwidge Dodgson, 1832–1898) in his *Alice in Wonderland*:

"Please would you tell me," said Alice a little timidly
. . . "why your cat grins like that?"
"It's a Cheshire cat," said the Duchess, "and that's
why."

To Let the Cat Out of the Bag: see *To Buy a Pig in a Poke*.

To Eat Crow: Meaning variously to eat one's words or to be forced into doing something unpleasant, this expression is said to have been born during the War of 1812. A tale told of that conflict has it that during a period of truce an American hunter accidentally crossed over into British-held territory and shot a crow. On hearing the shot, a British officer approached the American with an eye to punishing the man. The officer was unarmed and, by complimenting the intruder on his marksmanship and his handsome musket, managed to talk the American into handing over the gun for an admiring look, whereupon the Britisher accused him of trespassing and, at gunpoint, ordered him to take a bite out of the dead crow. When the officer (who apparently was not blessed with an overabundance of foresight) returned the musket, the American happily made him down the rest of the bird.

300Jim Crow: Coming from a minstrel-show song of the early 1800s, this is a derogatory term for blacks (an obvious reference to the bird's color) and, at one time, for renegades. Derived from it are such expressions as *jim crow laws* (regulations that prohibit the black from associating with whites or sharing in the privileges accorded them) and *jim crow cars* (railway carriages set aside for black use).

D

Dog Days: Referring to days of great heat, this expression comes from Roman times, when the people thought that the July rising of Sirius, the Dog Star, joined with the sun in adding to the summer warmth. To them the dog days were the hottest days of the summer and were called *caniculares dies*.

The Hair of the Dog That Bit You: Centuries old, this saying, as many a novice New Year's Eve celebrant has been told on his first morning-after, means that a hangover can best be cured by taking a drink of whatever it was that gave you the hangover. As British writer John Heywood put it back in the 1500s:

> I pray thee, let me and my fellows have a haire of the dog that bit us last night.
>
> —*Proverbs*

What the novice (and veteran) New Year's Eve celebrant likely does not know is that the saying is derived from an old folk remedy for a dog bite. The remedy called for burning a hair of the offending dog and then placing it on the wound.

Dog-rose: As a follow-up to the preceding entry, here is the common, wild rose that the Greeks thought able to cure the bite of a mad dog.

Donkey: This term originated in the 1700s to describe a dim-witted or silly person. The theory is that it came into being because polite conversation needed a substitute for *ass*, which had long meant the buttocks as well as a stupid person and had evolved into such vulgarisms as *asshole* (for a foolish individual as well as the anus). The new word may have been based on the animal's dun coloring.

E

Egghead: Once, for obvious reasons, a bald person. Today the term is more often used to describe an intellectual or a person of apparent cultural and artistic tastes. The two meanings are connected by the fact that intellectuals in earlier centuries were popularly depicted as bald or balding to the point where they had high fore-heads, which were thought to be a sign of intelligence.

White Elephant: A useless or burdensome posses-sion, often one too expensive to throw away. The term rises out of the tales of Siamese kings who used the al-bino elephant as a device for destroying courtiers who had displeased them. Once the elephant was presented, the expense of satisfying the animal's massive appetite drove the recipient to financial ruin. In Siam (Thailand) the albino elephant, because of its rarity, was considered sacred. It was the property of the king only and could be ridden, killed, or owned by another only with the king's consent. Out of the expression has come today's *white elephant sale*, meaning an informal sale of donated, un-wanted possessions and usually held by a church or club.

F

A Flea in the Ear: The British have traced this one to the fifteenth century, and the French to an even earlier time. Originally it meant to suffer a surprising, usually unpleasant experience, but today has the added meaning of receiving a hint or suggestion.

In its time the saying has also referred to someone suf-fering intense sexual desires. The sixteenth-century British adopted a variation—*to be sent off with a flea in the ear*—meaning to receive a severe scolding or harsh rebuff.

Flea Market: Meaning a market, usually open-air, at which secondhand merchandise is sold, with the impli-cation being that the merchandise is much used and thus filled with fleas, this term may have evolved from any of several sources—from the well-known Parisian second-hand mart *Le Marché aux Puces* (*puces* = fleas); from New York City's Fly Market, which flourished from be-fore the American Revolution to the early nineteenth cen-tury; or from the Dutch Vly or Vlie Market (*vly* or *vlie* = valley). It is thought that the New York City market took its name from the Dutch operation, with the change in spelling from *vly* to *fly* and thence to *flea* occurring because of the similarity of the three words.

He Eats No Fish: No longer heard, this saying was popular during the reign of England's Elizabeth I (1533–1603) when the enmity between Protestants and Roman Catholics was intense. At the time Protestants refused to follow the Catholic tradition of abstaining from meat on Friday. *He who eats no fish,* then, was someone whom Protestants considered honest and trustworthy because he had no part of Catholic ways.

Neither Fish Nor Fowl: Something whose nature cannot be classified, or someone of indefinite opinion. The term has been traced to the sixteenth century when England's King Henry broke with the Catholic Church. At the time the phrase was worded *neither fish nor flesh* and referred to someone who was neither Catholic (did not abstain from fish on days of fasting) nor Protestant (did not abstain from meat on similar days) and was therefore a person without any religious bent. Somewhere along the line the expression was extended to *neither fish, fowl, nor flesh,* a form in which it is sometimes heard today.

A Fly in the Ointment: Whenever we use this phrase to describe a trifling annoyance—as we often do—we're repeating something that dates back more than two thousand years, when it appeared in the Old Testament:

> Dead flies cause the ointment of the apothecary to send forth a stinking savor; so doth a little folly him that is in reputation for wisdom and honor.
>
> —Ecclesiastes

G

Goatee: A type of beard that covers only the chin and thus resembles the tufts of hair below the mouths of both male and female goats. This is an Americanism that was first heard in the mid-1800s, when "chin whiskers," as they were also called, were much in vogue. It became a facial feature in pictures of Uncle Sam in the late 1860s.

Billy Goat and Nanny Goat: The colloquial names for a male and female goat, respectively. Both date from sometime in the eighteenth century. Each combines the word *goat* with the diminutive form of a proper name— Billy for William and Nanny for Anne.

To Get One's Goat: Meaning to annoy or frustrate someone in the extreme, this is another American invention. Thought to have originated as recently as the late nineteenth or early twentieth century, it is connected with the longtime practice of Thoroughbred trainers to place a goat in the stall of a nervous racehorse because of the visitor's calming effect. The expression is said to have evolved from the shady gambling strategy of stealing the goat—getting the goat away—on the night before a race so that the horse would become so unnerved that his chances of victory would be greatly reduced.

To Kill the Goose That Laid the Golden Egg: Unlike the two preceding entries, this one is a genuine old-timer. Meaning to take a present gain in stupid exchange for the loss of a greater future reward, the expression comes from the ancient Greek tale of the man who owned a goose that magically laid golden eggs. The man killed the goose in the greedy hope of securing all of the animal's eggs at one time, only to find that he had put an end to the rich supply.

Goose Step: The military step in which the marchers swing their legs high from the hips while holding the knees in a locked position. Though most commonly associated with the German army of the Hitler era, the step dates back to the days of Frederick the Great (1712–1786). A source of widespread derision today, the step takes its name from its unmistakable, though highly exaggerated, similarity to the goose's straight-legged waddle. In Britain and other countries, a modified form of the goose step is to be seen in the formal slow step.

Grasshopper: This is a term with a variety of meanings. First and foremost, it is the name that has been applied since the thirteenth century to the small, plant-eating insects familiar to us all; the name combines their grass-green color and their jumping abilities. Today the term serves as the nickname for light, unarmed military scout aircraft and as the name of a mixed drink containing the greenish liqueur crème de menthe. There is also a *grasshopper pie*, a confection with a single crust made of crème de menthe or green-colored mint ice cream or a combination of the two.

Knee High to a Grasshopper: Referring to someone who is very small, usually a child, this phrase has been a familiar one in the United States since the mid-1800s. Prior to that time a small person was various dubbed *knee high to a bumblebee*, *a mosquito*, or *a splinter*.

H

Harebrained: Describing a foolhardy, silly, or insane person, this term is used interchangeably with hairbrained. Of the two hare-brained is by far the older, with its use occurring as early as the sixteenth century.

Harelip: A cleft in the upper lip, so called because it resembles the upper lip of a hare. In folklore the deformity is said to be caused at birth by a malicious elf or fairy.

Mad As a March Hare: It is likely that most people associate this expression, which describes an unbalanced or deranged person, with the delightfully wacky March Hare who attended the mad tea party in Lewis Carroll's *Alice in Wonderland*. Of the Hare Carroll wrote:

The March Hare will be much the more interesting, and perhaps, as this is May, it won't be raving mad— at least not so mad as it was in March.

As indicated in *Alice*, the expression stems from the

fact that hares had been seen to be especially wild in
March, their mating season. The expression, however,
was in use long before Carroll's day. It was a commonplace in the England of the 1500s and may even date back
to the 1300s. The Renaissance theologian Desiderius
Erasmus (ca. 1466–1536) wrote of the animals, but called
them "marsh hares." Though his terminology is suspected of having been in error, he might have chosen it
deliberately since he specifically pointed out that

> Hares are wilder in marshes from the absence of hedges
> and cover.
>
> —*Aphorisms*

Whatever the case, we now know that hares mate not just
in March but from January through August. Erasmus, however, was on the right track in his deduction about the "absence of hedges and cover." The hares' wild behavior is best
seen in March because they are no longer concealed by the
early darkness of deep winter and are yet to be hidden by the
thick foliage of spring and summer.

Hawks and Doves: Now used as a general expression to
distinguish those political leaders and citizens who favor war
or strong military action from those who favor peace or ne-
gotiations leading to peace, the terms are derived from the
characteristics of the respective animals—the strong, sharp-
eyed bird of prey and the creature whose timidity and gentleness long ago made it the symbol of peace. The expression
has been in widespread use in recent years to describe the
supporters and opponents of the Vietnam War, but its family
tree can be traced to the early nineteenth century, when the
term *warhawk* was introduced as a popular designation of
those Americans who agitated in favor of the War of 1812
against Great Britain.

To Draw a Red Herring Across One's Path: Meaning
a strategy intended to mislead someone or divert one's

attention from the main issue, this expression was heard as early as the seventeenth century in England, when gentlemen hunters used the strong odor of a smoked herring in training their dogs to follow a scent. The tactic was soon put to use by poachers. When up against pursuers with bloodhounds or hunting dogs, they pulled a smoked herring (whose color is changed to a reddish brown from its original silvery hue by the smoking process) across their paths to mislead the animals.

The strategy eventually led to the use of *red herring* as a convenient name for any diversionary measure. Prime examples of such measures are the false clues found in mystery novels. The term provided British mystery writer Dorothy L. Sayers (1893–1957) with the title for one of her most popular brain teasers, *Five Red Herrings*.

Hobbyhorse: A child's plaything today, the hobbyhorse got its start in the Middle Ages as a prop used in British Morris dancing, a type of folk dancing in which the participants represented figures from the Robin Hood legends. The horse, consisting of a wicker frame draped over with cloth, pranced and gamboled throughout the dance, thanks to a dancer concealed beneath its drapery. In time the structure of the horse was simplified and reduced to nothing more than a stick with a horse's head attached. As such it became a popular children's toy. In that form—and, more elaborately, as a model horse mounted on rockers (the rocking horse)—it has remained a favorite plaything to this day.

Horsepower: The rate of engine and motor power established by Scottish inventor and engineer James Watt (1736–1819) to indicate the power produced by his steam engine. Watt estimated that a strong dray horse could lift an average twenty-two thousand pounds per minute during an eight-hour day. He increased this average by fifty percent to account for the greater strength of his engine. Since then, horsepower has been recognized as being the equivalent of lifting thirty-three thousand pounds one foot in one minute.

I

Iron Horse: Heard only occasionally nowadays, this is the name invented for locomotives during the first years of their use in the early nineteenth century.

J

Jumbo: An elephant or an exceptionally large person. Jumbo was the name of an enormous elephant (he weighed in at some 6.5 tons) that was long a fixture at the London Zoo, where he gave rides to children. He was sold to American showman and circus owner P. T. Barnum in 1882 and was accidentally killed three years later when struck by a railroad engine.

K

Kangaroo Court: A mock trial (initially for jail inmates by their fellow prisoners) conducted in ignorance of proper judicial procedure. Because the kangaroo is native to Australia, the term is widely thought to have originated there, but is actually an American invention that has been in the language here since the mid-1800s. Whoever devised it is thought to have likened the kangaroo court's penchant for "jumping" to improper decisions to the animal's renowned jumping ability.

Kiwi: Slang for a New Zealander or, among aviators, a ground crewman. The reference is to the New Zealand bird that is unable to fly.

L

To Beard the Lion: To defy someone or to engage courageously in a face-to-face confrontation. This ancient phrase is found in the Old Testament story of how David pursued a lion who had stolen a lamb and

> . . . smote him, and delivered it (the lamb) out of his mouth: and when he rose against me, I caught him by his beard, and smote him, and slew him.
>
> —I Samuel

Lounge Lizard: We need go back only to the 1920s for this one's birth. It was the derogatory name given to young men who made their livings by dancing with or escorting wealthy, usually older, women about.

Lobsters: Had you lived at the time of the American Revolution, this would have been your slang word for the British soldiers in your midst, used because of their red jackets. The term, however, would not have been original to you or your fellow colonists. It dates back to the 1600s in England.

M

Build a Better Mousetrap: This one is credited to America's Ralph Waldo Emerson:

> If a man write a better letter, preach a better sermon, or make a better mousetrap than his neighbor, though he build his house in the woods, the world will still make a beaten path to his door.

N

To Lead About by the Nose: To be under the complete domination or at the beck and call of a stronger-willed individual. One of the few expressions in this glossary that does not refer specifically to an animal, it is nevertheless firmly rooted in animal lore. It is based in the age-old practice of leading tame and not-so-tame animals—cows, horses, camels, and bears—about by means of a tether fastened to their snouts. It goes back to biblical times.

The Swedish Nightingale: At times applied today to a woman with a fine singing voice (or sarcastically to one without), this was the name given to the noted Swedish soprano Jenny Lind (1820–1887) when she was introduced to the American public by impresario P. T. Barnum.

O

One-Horse Town: An Americanism that can be traced to the mid-1800s, but is strongly suspected of being of a much older origin. It initially meant a town so small that it needed just a single horse to carry out all its transportation needs. In recent years the phrase has been expanded to mean also a small and often amateurish enterprise, such as a *one-horse outfit* or a *one-horse show*.

P

The Pope's or Parson's Nose: Both are insulting comparisons with the rump of a fowl. The former came into use in the 1400s when the British, in the wake of the reign of James II, felt they were faced with the hated prospect of a Catholic monarch ascending to the throne. The *parson's nose* is an American variation that has been around since the early nineteenth century.

Pig Latin: Schoolchildren of old are credited with inventing this "language" to keep adults from understanding their private conversations. The youngsters communicated simply by moving the first consonant (or consonants) in a word to the end of the word and adding the sound *ay* to it; when a word opened with a vowel, the sound *ay* was still attached to the word ending. And so one youngster could let another know that he was conversant with the "language" by saying "Iay ancay eakspay igpay atinlay." No one knows when children first began to use the language, but its name is thought to have originated in England in the early 1900s, a time when most children were still being instructed in Latin.

Piggy Bank: A child's safe in the shape of a pig, this toy for the storage of coins has been on the scene in England since the early 1400s. It is thought, however, not to have had any connection with the pig at the time, but was an earthenware jar in which families kept spare coins. The Old English word for such a jar was *pygg*. Later in the 1400s the bank—with a few coins inside—was given by an employer to his workers as a Christmas gift. Somewhere along the line, the word *pygg* was altered to *piggy*, with the bank then taking the shape that it has retained to this day—that of a brightly colored piglet.

To Buy a Pig in a Poke: To make the mistake of purchasing any item of merchandise without first checking on its quality and condition. The phrase is British in origin, but the time of its invention is unknown. What can be said is that it dates back over the centuries to the time when *pig* meant a young swine still small enough to be carried to market in a *poke*, a little bag. Once there, some shrewd peasants would try to sell the animal to gullible customers without opening the poke—and would get away with the trick at times.

The French had a similar saying: *to buy a cat in a sack*. The astute purchaser who insisted on seeing the merchandise was responsible for an expression that is still with us today: *to let the cat out of the bag*. Today, the phrase means to reveal a secret, either deliberately or unwittingly.

In a Pig's Eye: Thought to be a blunt and impolite way of disagreeing with a person's opinion or claim, this expression is actually the epitome of courtesy when we find that it is the replacement for an early-twentieth-century phrase: *in a pig's ass*.

Pup Tent: This colloquialism for the wedge-shaped military and camping tent has been in use in the United States since the days of the Civil War. Along with the variant *dog tent*, it was invented because the tent obviously struck its occupants as being of a size that could better accommodate small animals than men.

Q

Quack: Variously, any kind of charlatan or a person who fraudulently professes medical knowledge. The former definition is the one mainly in use today. The latter was applied to ignorant or deceitful medical practitioners as early as the 1600s in Great Britain, with the word being an abbreviation of the old Dutch word *quacksalver* (now *kwakzalver*), meaning "puffer of salves," namely, a pretender to medical skills or a medical salesman who exaggerated the merits of his products.

The allied term, *quackery*, has long been slang for the practice or pretensions of the quack.

R

Round Robin: Though it contains the name of the beloved bird, this expression has nothing to do with the animal. Thought to have been devised by seamen sometime in the eighteenth or nineteenth century, it was a petition of grievance addressed to a ship's captain. The seamen, rather than signing the petition in descending order according to their roles in its creation, wrote their names in a circle around the statement, placing the signatures so that they resembled the spokes of a wheel. The ruse prevented the captain from identifying and punishing the instigators of the petition.

The original meaning of *round robin* remains in use to this day. It has, however, been joined by other definitions. It now also describes a contest in which every contestant meets every other contestant in turn, and a letter that, on being sent in turn to the members of the group, is signed by each (sometimes with an added comment) and then passed on to the next.

S

To Make Sheep's Eyes: To look gently and amorously at someone. British poet John Skelton (ca. 1460–1529) may have invented the expression when he wrote of what happens when "ye kyst sheep's ie" at a lady. Skelton apparently thought the sheep's eye was a gentle thing to behold. Prior to his time the British phrase for the bestowal of a loving look had been the blunt *to cast wanton eyes upon young women*.

Snake in the Grass: Describing someone who is a hidden enemy, this most commonplace of clichés is an abbreviation of a line written by the Roman poet Virgil. In his *Ecologues* he warned us to beware of anyone who is like a snake lurking in the grass. Today, the hidden enemy is often interpreted as one who pretends friendship.

Swan Song: Meaning today the final appearance or work by a noted personality, here, indeed, is one of the oldest of all animal expressions. It comes from the ancients, who believed that the swan was mute until the moments before its death, at which time it broke into song. Greek legend holds that the song was a joyous one because the swan was sacred to Apollo, the god of music and poetry, and knew that its approaching death would unite it with its beloved deity.

The Greeks also believed that the souls of dead poets were placed in the bodies of swans.

To Cast Pearls Before Swine: There is nothing here to match the beauty behind the idea of the swan song. Bluntly telling you that you are wasting your time and energy when you attempt to offer ''pearls of wisdom'' to an unappreciative and heedless person, the remark was voiced by Christ in his Sermon on the Mount and was directed against the Philistines:

> Neither cast ye your pearls before swine, lest they trample them under their feet.
>
> —Matthew

T

Paper Tiger: A person or an organization that appears to be strong but is actually weak. The term is thought to be of ancient Chinese origin. It became a part of Western speech in 1946 when Mao Tse-tung (1893–1976), then the chief of the Communist Chinese Army and later the founder and chairman of the People's Republic of

China, told a visiting correspondent that the world's anticommunist forces were *paper tigers*.

To Talk Turkey: To speak plainly and simply, especially when handing out advice or criticism. The expression is an American one and has been traced to the early 1800s. No one knows exactly when or how it came into use, but one widely told and much varied folk story has it that it was born during a brief conversation between a white man and an Indian who had gone hunting together and had bagged a turkey and a buzzard. When the time came to divide their kill, the white man engaged in some fast talk in the hope of having the turkey go to him. The Indian nodded calmly and then said that he had been listening to the white hunter "talk turkey to me" and that it was now his, the Indian's, turn to "talk turkey to you."

If the story has any truth to it, then the term was early used in a manner not intended by the Indian. Throughout the nineteenth century it meant to speak openly but pleasantly to a person. Some authorities think that at the time the expression pertained specifically to any young man who became so embarrassed when speaking to a pretty young thing that his words tumbled out in an unintelligible flood that resembled the gobbling sounds made by the turkey.

Only in our century has it come to mean straight and blunt talk.

Cold Turkey: Prior to the time that *to talk turkey* assumed its present meaning, the expression *to talk cold turkey* was employed for speaking bluntly and looking facts squarely in the face. Though the phrase is heard but rarely nowadays, the term *cold turkey* itself remains known to all, meaning as it does to quit smoking, drinking, or using drugs on the spur of the moment, without any time taken for preparation. It came into use sometime in the 1920s.

W

Weasel Out: To avoid a commitment or to find a way not to follow through on a commitment. An Americanism, the term has been in use since the 1920s and is based on the furtiveness of the weasel, a diminutive, sharply clawed rodent whose size enables it to pass easily through small openings.

Weasel Words: Conveniently ambiguous words or a statement in which the wording obscures the original meaning. The expression refers to the weasel's liking for bird's eggs and seems to have been born in 1900, in a political article published by *Century Magazine*. The article contained the following sentence:

> "Why, weasel words are words that suck the life out of the words next to them, just as the weasel sucks the eggs and leaves the shell.
> —Stewart Chaplin, "Stained Glass Political Platform"

Chaplin may have given the expression its start, but Theodore Roosevelt clarified its meaning and made it nationally popular in a 1916 speech attacking President Woodrow Wilson's stance on military conscription prior to World War I:

> You can have universal training, or you can have voluntary training, but when you use the word *voluntary* to qualify the word *universal*, you are using a weasel word; it has sucked all the meaning out of *universal*. The two words flatly contradict each other.

Mr. Roosevelt must have liked the expression because he turned to it again in a speech delivered later in 1916:

> When a weasel sucks an egg, the meat is sucked out of the word; and if you use a weasel word after another word there is nothing left of the other.

Pop Goes the Weasel: Contrary to popular belief, this song is thought to have nothing to do with the rodent. Nor, though it has been a popular children's song for more than a century, was it intended for youngsters but for adults when first published in 1853:

Up and down the City Road
In and out the Eagle
That's the way the money goes,
Pop goes the weasel.

The song has long been regarded as one for children because of its nonsense lyrics. Only when you learn their origin do the words make sense and you realize they were never intended for tender little ones. The City Road in the song is a main thoroughfare in London, and the Eagle was a nineteenth-century pub and music hall standing somewhere along its length. The pub was a popular haunt for Saturday-night drinkers who, if they wished to continue the evening's merriment after sliding all their money across the bar, had to leave for a time so that they could *pop*—pawn—the weasel. And what was the weasel? No one is quite certain, but it is widely thought to have been a slang term for a household flatiron whose narrowness reminded people of the rodent's face.

Actually, this is just one explanation given the lyrics. Some authorities feel that the words may indeed concern the rodent, theorizing that *pop* refers to the weasel's active movements. There is also the theory that *pop* has a sexual connotation to it.

Bibliography

Ammer, C., *It's Raining Cats and Dogs . . . and Other Beastly Expressions*. New York: Paragon House, 1989.

Batchelor, J. F., and De Lys, C., *Superstitious? Here's Why*. New York: Harcourt Brace, 1954.

Berry, P. D., and Repass, M. E., *Grandpa Says . . . Superstitions and Sayings*. Louisa, Kentucky: Printed by Billingsley Printing & Engraving, Fredericksburg, Virginia, 1980.

Blumenthal, S., *Black Cats and Other Superstitions*. Milwaukee: Raintree, 1977.

Bohle, B., *The Home Book of American Quotations*. New York: Dodd Mead, 1967.

Bombaugh, C. C., *Gleanings for the Curious From the Harvest Fields of Literature: A Mélange of Excerpta*. Hartford, Connecticut; Cincinnati, and St. Louis: A. D. Worthington and A. G. Nettleton Companies, 1875.

Campbell, J., *The Masks of God: Occidental Mythology*. New York: Penguin Books, 1976.

———, *The Masks of God: Primitive Mythology*. New York: Penguin Books, 1976.

Cavendish, R., Editor, *Man, Myth and Magic*, 24 volumes. New York: Cavendish Corporation, 1970.

Emrich, D., *Folklore on the American Land*. Boston: Little, Brown, 1972.

Emrich, M. V., and Korson, G., *The Child's Book of Folklore: American Songs, Games, Riddles, Tales, Rhymes, Beliefs and Customs*. New York: Dial, 1947.

Evans, I. H., Editor, *Brewer's Dictionary of Phrase and Fable*. New York: Harper & Row, 1981.

Fergussen, R., *The Penguin Dictionary of Proverbs*. Harmondsworth, Middlesex, England: Penguin Books, 1983.

Fisher, M.F.K., *A Cordiall Water: A Garland of Odd and Old Receipts to Assuage the Ills of Man and Beast*. San Francisco: North Point Press, 1981.

Gaffney, S., and Cashman, S., Editors, *Proverbs and Sayings of Ireland*. Portmarnock, County Dublin, Ireland: Wolfhound Press, 1974.

Graves, R., *The Greek Myths*, 2 volumes. Baltimore: Penguin Books, 1955.

Haggard, H. W., M.D., *Devils, Drugs, and Doctors: The Story of Healing from Medicine-Man to Doctor*. New York: Harper & Row, 1979.

Hamilton, E., *Mythology: Timeless Tales of Gods and Heroes*. New York: New American Library, 1940.

Hand, W. D., Editor, *American Folk Medicines*. Berkeley: University of California Press, 1976.

Harrowen, J., *The Origins of Rhymes, Songs, and Sayings*. London: Kaye and Ward, 1977.

Humphreys, W. J., *Weather Proverbs and Paradoxes*. Baltimore: Williams & Wilkins, 1923.

Jobes, G., *Dictionary of Mythology Folklore and Symbols*, 2 volumes. New York: Scarecrow Press, 1962.

Johnson, C., *What They Say in New England*. New York: Columbia University Press, 1963.

Kirk, G. S., *Myth: Its Meaning and Functions in Ancient and Other Cultures*. London and Berkeley: Cambridge University Press and University of California Press, 1970.

Komroff, M., Selected by, *The Great Fables of all Nations*. New York: Tudor, 1936.

Leach, M., Editor, *Funk & Wagnalls Standard Dictionary of Folklore Mythology and Legend*. New York: Funk and Wagnalls, 1984.

Lee, A., *Weather Wisdom*. Garden City, New York: Doubleday, 1977.

Magill, F. N., Editor, *Magill's Quotations in Context*, 2 volumes. New York: Salem Press, 1969.

New Larousse Encyclopedia of Mythology. New York: Crown, 1989.

Perl, L., *Don't Sing Before Breakfast, Don't Sleep in the Moonlight: Everyday Superstitions and How They Began*. New York: Clarion Books, 1988.

Radford, E., and M. A. (Edited and revised by Christina Hole), *Encyclopedia of Superstitions*. London: Hutchinson of London, 1961.

Robinson, H. S., and Wilson, K., *Myths and Legends of All Nations*. Garden City, New York: Doubleday, 1960.

Schwartz, A., *Cross Your Fingers, Spit in Your Hat*. Philadelphia: J. B. Lippincott, 1974.

Smith, W. G., *The Oxford Dictionary of English Proverbs*. London: Oxford University Press, 1970.

Steele, P. W., *Ozark Tales and Superstitions*. Gretna, Louisiana: Pelican, 1988.

Stevenson, B., *The Home Book of Proverbs, Maxims and Familiar Quotations*. New York: Macmillan, 1948.

Tallman, M. *Dictionary of American Folklore*. New York: Philosophical Library, 1959.

Taylor, A., and Whiting, B. J., *A Dictionary of American Proverbs and Proverbial Phrases, 1820–1880*. Cambridge: Belknap Press of Harvard University Press, 1958.

Walsh, W. S., *Curiosities of Popular Customs and of Rites, Ceremonies, Observations, and Miscellaneous Antiquities*. Philadelphia: J. B. Lippincott, 1898; Detroit: Gale Research, 1966.

Index

193

About the Author

A professional writer all his adult life, Edward F. Dolan has more than eighty books to his credit on subjects ranging from history and biography to sports and recreation. Prior to devoting himself full-time to book writing, he worked as a newspaper reporter, an editor, and a teacher. He and his wife live in Novato, California.